How To Coach
Little League Baseball

By Mickey McConnell

www.sunvillagepublications.com

How To Coach Little League Baseball
By Mickey McConnell

Copyright © 2010

No part of this publication may be reproduced, stored in a retrieval system or transmitted in any form or by any means, electronic, mechanical, photocopying, recording or otherwise, without prior written permission from the publisher.

Disclaimer: Neither the author nor the publisher accepts any responsibility for any injury, damage, or unwanted or adverse circumstances or conditions arising from use or misuse of the material contained within this publication. While every effort has been made to ensure reliability and accuracy of the information within, the liability, negligence or otherwise, or from any use, misuse or abuse arising the operation of any methods, strategies, instructions or ideas contained in the material herein is the sole responsibility of the reader.

Cover Image Credits © Lucian Coman/Dreamstime.com

Cover design by www.WebCopyAlchemy.com

Foreword

The combination of baseball knowledge and enthusiasm for teaching it is an ideal foundation for an instruction book.

Mickey McConnell possesses such a foundation and to a degree sufficient to make this volume a valuable addition to the library of both coach and player.

The author's baseball knowledge has been gained from many years of on-the-field association with players in the major and minor leagues, on college fields and countless sandlot diamonds. The scope of his travels as a scout, instructor, and supervisor of clinic and tryout camp includes Latin America and the Orient. The following pages reflect this broad and unique background.

There is far more to teaching baseball than merely telling "how to." McConnell, who writes for the beginner as well as the coach, reflects this understanding by dealing with the would-be player's attitudes and disposition. He delves into the many intangibles that so heavily influence success or failure at bat and in the field.

I have known Mickey McConnell for many years, and always as a sincere and indefatigable worker in behalf of baseball. These fine qualities and more are reflected in a baseball instruction book that should be, and will be, I am sure, welcomed wherever the great game is played.

BRANCH RICKEY

Preface

This is the official Little League book of instruction for boys beginning to play baseball, and particularly for the adults who supervise and coach them. Its purpose is to demonstrate the correct techniques of play and to outline methods of motivation and practice procedures, which have proved to be constructive and successful.

The concentration is on the fundamentals of running, throwing, fielding, batting, and team play to enable the youngsters to play the game better and, in so doing, to gain the sense of achievement which comes from acquiring a skill and to enjoy participation under safe conditions. The proper ways to slide, to field ground and fly balls, to throw to bases and tag runners, to make the double play, to pitch, and to catch are clearly explained and illustrated through action pictures. Bunting leads into batting, and sprinting ties in with base running. Effective fielding drills to improve the skills while maintaining the interest of the players are covered, as well as the use and construction of simple training aids.

Throughout the book the values of baseball in developing healthy attitudes of sportsmanship, citizenship, teamwork, hustle, fitness, and application are emphasized.

Although the larger part of the material is directly applicable to the youthful player, such subjects as the value of an education to an athlete can best be interpreted in the individual situation by the adult manager, coach, or parent. Similarly, the material about leadership, safety, spring training, building a team, the batting order, fielding drills, training aids, coaching on the base lines, and setting an example will be of primary interest and value to the people who guide the boys in Little League and similar baseball programs for boys.

MICKEY MCCONNELL

Williamsport, Pa.

Table of Contents

1. Leadership 3
2. Safety First, Last, and Always 12
3. Spring Tryouts 14
4. Building a Team 19
5. Running and Sliding 23
6. Batting and Bunting 34
7. The Batting Order 48
8. Infield Play 51
9. Outfield Play 68
10. Catching 76
11. Pitching 89
12. Fielding Drills 108
13. Coaching and Signals 115
14. Training Aids 121
15. Fitness Isn't Seasonal 126
16. An Education Helps 134
17. Setting an Example 139

    Index 143

1

Leadership

This is a book for managers, coaches, players, and parents. While it is written primarily for the beginner in baseball—the Little Leaguer—the reader will discover that the same fundamentals work in all branches of baseball. The right way to execute a play and the right attitude get the same results in the major leagues as in the Little Leagues, and the wrong way is just as inimical to good results.

The surprising thing is that so many major leaguers make mistakes—correctible mistakes—which proves that we shouldn't expect too much of boys and that we should always remember that it is human to err. At the same time, we should never lose sight of the opportunity to teach fundamentals of play and of constructive living.

It was Herbert Hoover who observed that team sports are the greatest training in morals, second only to religious faith, and one of the greatest stimulants of constructive joy in the world. We can provide this joy and be a part of it if we realize the potentialities of a program like Little League and make the most of them.

Most of us are not great athletes and few of us have been professional players and coaches, but years of observation will convince the candid reader of the truth of Branch Rickey's conviction that any man with normal intelligence and a desire to learn can become a capable baseball coach or manager. Willingness to learn and to lead are key factors in the success of the program.

One coach described this reaction: "You'd be amazed at the trust these youngsters put in you. They think you're the greatest fellow on earth. You get a funny feeling when you realize they are following you around, trying to be like you and act like you."

The relationship between players of all ages and managers or coaches is far better than the usual relationship between learner and instructor. Elton

True blood, the noted author and philosopher, has observed that the coach and player are on the same side: "The coach does not seem to the student to be one who is primarily his judge, but rather one who, at every possible point, is seeking to assist him to do better. They are partners in a single thrilling effort. If the coach is a man of character, his influence on the lives of the players is both beneficent and strong."

Many managers and coaches know from experience that Little Leaguers are very impressionable. As coaches, they can be a strong force for good if they take advantage of their opportunities for constructive leadership. For example, a beginner can learn something new about the game every day. It may be such a simple thing as how to grip the bat or where to stand in the batter's box, and you may have to repeat the lesson again and again. However, the youngster will leave the field with real satisfaction if you can remind him that he learned something new today and thus is a better player than he was yesterday.

KNOW YOUR PLAYERS. If you get to know your boys, their physical limitations and capabilities, their environment and their personalities, you will

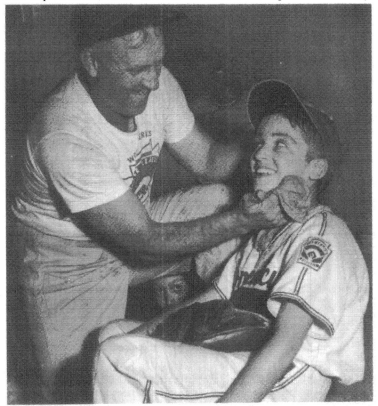

FIG. 1. Managers and players should build a relationship of friendship, understanding, and respect.

be able to help them grow and develop. Thus you may find a boy whose parents take little interest in him and who has limited ability. A little praise will give a big boost to his morale. Remember that boys have a short interest span. Vary your instruction program and keep it fun.

To serve youngsters well, you must know their needs, interests, and ability, and you must know your own limitations, too.

ATTITUDES ARE IMPORTANT. Perhaps the greatest opportunity comes to the adult leader in developing attitudes. Since his own attitude will be reflected by a majority of his players, it is important that he understand and instruct that the relationships with umpires, managers, coaches, and other players should be a friendly one.

Keep in mind that players should participate for the enjoyment and benefit they derive. Too often the tendency is to shower attention and awards on the talented lad and to ignore the benchwarmer. Achievement is its own reward, and a boy who hits a home run gets sufficient satisfaction from performing that feat. He doesn't need additional honors.

Too often on the playing field participants develop an escapist complex by blaming defeat on the officials, team-mates, or "dirty work at the crossroads." Youngsters should learn that the best teams don't win all the time-even when they put forth their best efforts—and that the worst teams don't lose all the time. There are days when the pennant-winning team gets the bad bounces, all the close plays go against it, and "bloop" hits land between the fielders. The team that continues to hustle from day to day, profits by its mistakes and learns not to repeat them, and learns to accept the fact that the "breaks" will even up over a season is the team with the right mental approach to the game. It has come to recognize that a majority of games can be decided by good or bad play on the field and by the type of leadership provided, and it conducts itself accordingly.

Players must learn that no one is successful in every effort—that they don't have any reason to regret a loss if they have performed to the best of their ability without violating the rules of the game or good sportsmanship—and that results may be different the next time if they continue to put forth their best efforts.

It is important for players to recognize the role of the umpire. You teach respect for law and order when you teach your players to respect the umpire and his role in the game. The only time the decision of an umpire should be questioned is when a manager or coach believes that the umpire has made a mistake in interpreting a rule or has not been able to see a play (such as a half-swing, or a trapped or juggled ball). Then the umpire should be asked in a courteous manner to check his rule book or to consult with another umpire who might have had a better view of the play.

Again, point out to your players that any close play may bring divided opinions between the contestants as to the outcome. This is entirely natural in a competitive situation, and because the umpire is nonpartisan, he is in a position to judge the play from a neutral viewpoint.

We must recognize, however, that the best and most experienced umpires make mistakes, just as players make errors and managers and coaches use poor judgment on occasion. Players must learn to accept the fact that no one is perfect, but that over a season of play as many decisions on questionable plays will be called in their favor as against them.

WE CAN LEARN FROM JAPAN. Before each National High School Baseball Tournament in Japan, all the players salute the tournament director and pledge in unison to play to the best of their ability, to be thankful for the opportunity to participate, to respect the officials and their opponents, and to play in such a way that they will strive to bring honor to their family, school, and country by playing according to the rules and the spirit of fair play. The teams bow to the "honorable" umpires and the umpires bow to the "honorable" players before and after every game to show that they appreciate the part each plays in making the game possible.

Cooperation is so important in life today that one of the great values of baseball comes from playing with other members of the team. Players soon understand that the success of a double play depends on the player who fields and throws the ball, the pivot man who takes the relay at second base and sends the ball on its way, and the player who stretches to catch it at first base.

In stressing the democratic values of team games Lynn McCraw of the University of Texas, writing in *Scholastic Coach,* points to cooperation, the opportunity for free competition, the voluntary submission to duly elected authority, and obedience to the law of the people:

> This obedience is not induced by fear of reprisal, but stems from a willingness to abide by what has been accepted as right and good for the common welfare. This is likewise a willingness to accept the decision of an impartial judge in settling all matters of dispute. The value of games in developing a respect for law and authority is truly immeasurable. Both coaches and players recognize that the rules are for the common good and represent the thinking of their representatives.

With good leadership, a youngster learns much more than the game itself. In Little League play he comes to realize the necessity for adequate preparation if one is to excel in any worthwhile activity. The boy is exposed to the humbling realization that everyone is endowed with varying degrees of natural talent, but that success usually comes to those who work the hardest. While developing a competitive spirit—the "will to win"—he simultaneously develops the perseverance to keep trying no matter what the score may be because the game isn't over until the final out.

Leadership 7

FIG. 2. Boys learn more than the fundamentals of play under good leadership.

HUSTLE IS A NECESSITY. One of the biggest favors a field leader can do for his players is to teach them to hustle. Players, officials, and spectators enjoy a game in which everyone hustles, with players running on and off the field, batters ready to take their turn at: bat, coaches in their coaching boxes as their team comes to bat, an extra catcher available to warm up the pitcher if necessary, a substitute player designated to retrieve bats promptly, and even the batter instructed to pick up the mask and hand it to the catcher on the other team if this will help to speed up play.

No one enjoys seeing a game in which the players walk on their heels and seem to be simply going through the motions. Not only does a lack of hustle destroy interest in the game, but it can drag out a game so long that a contest which begins when visibility is good cannot continue without endangering the participants, or can result in the umpire halting the game because of darkness.

It can also cause a player to reach his saturation point of interest. A few years ago sloppy play, poor organization and leadership, lack of control by pitchers, and hot, humid weather made a twilight game seem interminable. The catcher for one team was an alert, aggressive lad who tried to keep his team alive. All of a sudden in the sixth inning he turned around and walked to the backstop to retrieve a wild pitch while the runner who represented the winning run sped from first to third base for the opposing team. This kind of play could cause an inexperienced manager to blow a fuse, but this boy was doing what came naturally.

Little Leaguers have not gained so much control of mind over body that they will drive themselves to exhaustion. No group of youngsters of Little League age would row themselves into a hospital as the Yale University crew did to win the Olympic crew races in Australia. When Little Leaguers grow tired, you may expect them to cease to put forth their best efforts. Child experts know that this is a normal reaction. It will rarely happen, however, if games are properly organized and if there is motivation to put sufficient hustle into the play to keep it interesting.

RAZZING IS OUT. Remember that it is against the rules and the spirit of Little League for you or your players to razz or heckle your opponents. Equally important, the boys should not be permitted to criticize other players on their own team, but should be taught to encourage them. And keep in mind that your players will respect you if you correct their mistakes in a quiet, friendly way rather than ranting and raving at them. Little Leaguers are receptive to ideas and instructions—and building confidence through friendly persuasion will work wonders with most boys.

A veteran manager has discovered that "at least one boy in every group seems to develop leadership when given the opportunity to do so." Such a boy can help immeasurably in setting a good pattern for others to follow. As in adult life, you will find good leaders and good followers on the baseball field if you look for them.

In teaching, there is a great temptation to try to teach beginners a dozen things at once. Concentrate on one thing at a time until a boy has mastered it. Otherwise you will only succeed in confusing your players. Keep in mind that all boys don't learn at the same speed or have the same capacity to retain learning. Yet patience can pay big dividends with some slow learners.

If you have a boy who can't concentrate, try to find a place for him on the team where he will get plenty of action so that he won't have time to "daydream." Remind him frequently of the game situation and what he should be prepared to do on the next play.

You can influence boys to develop good health habits—enough sleep, a balanced diet, when to exercise in relation to the game and practice schedule. (For instance, a boy shouldn't spend the morning pitching batting practice on a sandlot or the afternoon swimming before pitching a twilight game in Little League.) If a boy has been ill, check with his parents or doctor to determine whether he is ready to play again and under what conditions.

Once in a while a manager may be faced with a disciplinary problem. A player may deliberately try to "cheat on the rules" or run over a smaller defensive player while running the bases in an effort to knock the ball out of his opponent's hands. There is no place for this type of thing in Little League, and you must take a firm stand against such tactics even to the point of benching a boy if he repeats such actions. Every effort should be made to correct players without holding them up to ridicule before[1] their teammates.

DEVELOP ALL PLAYERS. You will build morale by developing all of your players—not just the nine or ten best boys. The day may come when several of your players are absent, and you will be in trouble if you haven't given your reserve players "game experience." Every manager can find a way to play all of his players at regular intervals, and he will have a stronger and happier team at the end of the season and in forthcoming seasons if he gives all of the boys a chance to play and develop.

To serve your team, you should know that you must give freely of your time and energy and that you may be subject to criticism from parents and other second guessers, but that your associations with these youngsters will keep you young in mind and spirit. The dedicated leader continually explores avenues of doing the job better and grows through the process of self-education. He seeks the advice of professional teachers and coaches, child psychologists, pediatricians, and similar experts, and he makes an effort to read the available publications which might give him new insights in his efforts.

For instance a study of Clarence G. Moser's excellent book *Understanding Boys* will provide insight about how boys are developing and about their need for training in physical skills, for building friendships and membership in a group, for opportunity and stimulation to improve and display motor abilities, for recognition of individual shortcomings and adjustments to them, and for understanding and sympathy from adults.

The dividends for making these extra efforts to prepare for leadership come to the manager through the privilege of building better boys through baseball.

WHY FUNDAMENTALS?

Why is it important for a boy to learn the fundamentals of the game of baseball? In the words of Arthur A. Esslinger, a prominent leader in physical education, "The benefits which boys can derive from playing baseball depend largely upon the skill and ability they develop in the sport. But first, they must be taught the correct fundamentals and must master these basic skills." Thus they play the game better and gain the sense of achievement that comes from improving their abilities.

It is possible to perfect baseball skills and at the same time to avoid injury. In fact the possession of skills helps to prevent accidents. Very seldom do we hear of a player who executes a play properly being injured. The man who knows how to throw, and uses this knowledge in throwing, doesn't pull a muscle in his arm, and the fellow who knows how to slide and uses this knowledge doesn't sprain an ankle or strain an elbow.

It is important that every player concentrate on the basic fundamentals. For instance, one can be so absorbed in swinging a bat hard in an effort to hit the ball out of the park that he never learns how to get maximum power through such things as balance, the short stride and hip pivot, the level shoulders and hips, and the level swing with complete follow-through.

In the following pages fundamentals of play are set forth to aid you in helping the boy who is beginning his career on the diamond. These are first fundamentals, and when they are mastered, the player is ready for refinements of play he sometimes sees displayed in major league games.

Every effort has been made to apply scientific principles to the techniques of play to be sure that the best methods, practices, and procedures are recommended. John Bunn, the brilliant coach and analyst, stated in his book *Scientific Principles of Coaching:*

> I have been disturbed by the tendency in others to accept blindly the methods employed by the star athlete and to assume that these methods are correct merely because the man is a top performer. By the same token, the methods taught by the successful coach are often considered to be the last word because that particular coach has a winning team. Few seem to question or inquire into the methods, or to consider the possibility that the star athlete or the championship team may be successful in spite of the methods employed.

Remember that some major leaguers are such remarkable athletes that they can use methods not recommended by the finest coaches and still be successful, but that players who get the best results try to improve their play, listen to their coaches, and study the game. Always keep in mind that if a game is worth playing it is worth playing to the best of the boy's ability.

And finally, don't forget Dr. Esslinger's advice: "A sense of humor is a wonderful asset to any manager. It is a safeguard against undue tensions and severities of unwise discipline. An overly serious atmosphere takes the fun and happiness out of Little League. After all, it is a game as far as the boys are concerned." It isn't Little League if it isn't fun.

AN AMERICAN TRADITION. Baseball for boys, properly conducted, becomes an enjoyable experience for all concerned, an asset and an inspiration to the community in which it is played.

In this push-button age when leisure can become a curse as well as a blessing and when physical fitness as well as mental fitness are major concerns, President Dwight D. Eisenhower has said: "Parents and adults working in Little League can improve and extend leadership in this important field. To maintain this fine American tradition with its contribution to the nation's health and ideals of fair play, we must continue to encourage our boys to take an active part in the game." This book is dedicated to that goal.

2

Safety First, Last, and Always

The safety factor is an important one at all levels of baseball, but it is particularly necessary with beginners. It should not be overlooked at any stage of Little League activity, whether in spring training, tryouts, practice sessions, or games. Coaches and managers might like to post the following list of precautions in a dugout, clubhouse, or dressing room:

1. Have an adult at the field at least a half hour in advance of the scheduled activity to control the group until the start of organized activity.

2. Check the field for obstacles—holes in outfield, stones, a hole in front of pitching rubber, etc.

3. Have the adult space the youngsters who are warming up so that other groups are not endangered by wild throws and muffed catches. The throwing should be parallel.

4. Unless the area is unusually large, have the adult keep the boys from participating in batting practice until the regular workouts begin. Pepper games can be organized if the players are spaced properly, with groups batting the ball parallel to each other. There should be no more than four players in each pepper game.

5. Have boys bring a jacket or sweater to wear during warm-up and after workout.

6. Require batters to wear batting helmets during batting practice. Helmets must be worn by batters and base-runners during games.

7. To keep bats from slipping out of batters' hands, use non-slip grips of tape on the handles, or have players use rosin on their hands.

8. Have rules about retrieving foul balls batted into busy streets.

9. The head-first slide should be prohibited except when returning to a base.

10. During sliding practice, bases should be left untied when boys are being taught the fundamentals of sliding.

Safety First, Last, and Always

11. Build a warning track at least six feet out from the fences and back stop, using cinders, gravel, or some similar material.

12. Inspect equipment regularly—particularly batting helmets and catching equipment.

13. Teach players to take good care of all equipment and facilities.

14. Players should not wear watches or rings.

ADDITIONAL SAFEGUARDS

1. Medical examinations should be given to all players prior to the opening of the season.

2. Whenever possible, a physician or nurse should be in attendance at each game.

3. All participants should be covered by accident insurance.

4. Each team should possess a first-aid kit, which should be complete and available at every game. It should be in the charge of someone trained to use it.

5. Preseason first-aid instruction should be given all managers and coaches each year.

6. All protective equipment should be of good quality and should fit properly.

7. All dugouts should be screened.

8. All players not participating in the game must remain in the dugouts.

9. Players should be taught the proper techniques of sliding, hitting, fielding, etc.

10. Equipment should not be left on the ground where it can be stepped on and injury result.

FIRST-AID KIT. Contents of the first-aid kit should include:

2 Bandages 1" x 10 yd.	33 Band-Aid plastic strips
2 Bandages 2" x 10 yd.	1 Burn ointment
1 Bandage 3" x 10 yd.	3 Ammonia inhalants
1 Cotton ½ oz.	1 Scissors
1 Adhesive tape 1" x 2½ yds.	1 Antiseptic
1 Gauze 1 yd.	1 First-Aid guide booklet
12 Sterile gauze pads 2" x 2"	6 Sterile eye pads
1 Triangular bandage	

3

Spring Tryouts

Several important contributions can be made to your league through a good tryout program in the spring. In the first place, there is little doubt that even the most talented and experienced baseball scout can be mistaken about the ability of a player when he fails to use a stop watch to check running speed or a tape measure to check the distance of a hit. Judgment remains an important factor, but the less guessing you have to do, the more likely you are to be correct in your evaluation of playing skills.

In the second place, it is of prime importance to convince the boys that they are being judged on their ability to run, throw, bat, and field and that there is equality of opportunity for every boy who becomes a candidate for a team. To parents who are likely to feel that their boy has more ability than another youngster—particularly if their boy isn't picked for a regular team and the other youngster is selected—you need an answer which must make sense to any fair-minded adult.

If one boy runs faster than another and you have a record of the running speeds, if he throws the ball farther and more accurately and these items have been recorded, if he can hit the ball farther off a batting tee and you measure the distance, you have something more than opinion as a basis for your selection. This can do much to convince the community that the players are picked because of their ability and for no other reason!

The suggestions that follow on testing youngsters at spring tryout sessions come from the vast experience of physical education leaders and of leagues throughout the world. Divide squads by ages with no more than 30 boys to a group. Bring out one group for a two-hour tryout, and then the remaining players in 30-boy groups until all have been tested. Have them warm up properly by throwing and running before beginning the workout.

RUNNING

Since it is a part of both offense and defense, running is the most important factor in baseball. Everything else being equal, take the boy who runs the fastest. Have three boys run together while using three stop watches in recording their speed. If they are Little Leaguers, the distance of the race should be 120 feet, and they should run 180 feet if they play on adult-sized diamonds.

If the choice of a candidate comes down to running speed and two boys have the same speed recorded on the watches, check the boys for running form. If one boy has good running form and the other bad form, select the boy who doesn't know how to run because coaching should improve his speed. Of course, there could be a rare exception to this rule if a boy is so awkward that it seems obvious that he would have great difficulty in learning how to run properly.

THROWING

In testing the throwing arm of an outfielder, have the boy throw from home plate toward center field. Outfielders should learn to throw "line drives" and should throw the ball with an overhand motion. (If possible, teach the players to throw the ball so that it will have a backward rotation such as an overhand pitcher uses in throwing a fast ball and a catcher should use in throwing to bases. This rotation will make the ball carry farther in the air and will make it bounce straight.)

It is important to start the boys out in this pattern since it is the proper one and will help to improve their throwing. Have them throw three times and measure the throws. You can stretch strings parallel to home plate or make chalk lines (in advance) 20 feet apart, starting 100 feet from home plate in Little League, to simplify the measuring process. Older players should throw from a distance of at least 150 feet. Throwing for accuracy is also very important, so have each player throw five times from the pitching distance at a strike zone target.

Once the players have been tested in throwing for distance and accuracy, have the infielders go through a fielding drill, throwing from the positions they want to play. After they have thrown from their chosen positions, have all of them throw from "the hole" at shortstop to determine the strength of their arms. Everything else being equal, the boy with the strongest arm should be the shortstop. (Of course, a left-handed boy would be an exception to this rule since first base is the only infield position he can play without handicapping himself.)

THROWING FROM THE HOLE. "The hole" at shortstop is a spot approximately halfway between shortstop and third base and approximately 10 feet back of the base line, where the top-notch shortstop will come up with the ball and occasionally make the long throw to first base. All long throws from shortstop and third base should be made with the overhand motion and rotation described for the outfield throw.

When testing the throwing arms of the infielders, attention should also be given to the agility and coordination of the boys. Good hands are important to infielders. They should have that quality which might be described as "glue in their gloves," since a fumbled ball can be disastrous. This attribute of good hands is particularly important to the shortstop and to the first baseman.

In checking the throwing arm of the catcher, have him make the throw to second base from behind home plate. Youngsters have a tendency to "crow hop" before they throw, and the boy who makes the longest hop before throwing the ball might display the strongest arm unless all the boys throw from the same spot. Do not eliminate left-handed candidates for the catching position or boys who wear glasses! However, the boy who wears glasses should be given extra protection through the use of glasses recommended by a doctor and the use of a rugged and roomy mask.

When the boys have been tested at the positions they prefer, they can be switched to other positions where they might be more successful. Try moving a left-handed shortstop to first base or the outfield, or switching a short boy with small hands from first base to the outfield and a tall boy with large hands from the outfield to first base.

CHOOSING PITCHERS

These throwing tests for distance and accuracy can be very important in evaluating pitching prospects. If you find a boy who has a strong and accurate arm, it is logical to assume that he is a pitching prospect.

Perhaps the most difficult assignment is that of cutting down the squad of pitchers. At the adult age level this is not such a problem since the pitchers can be checked on their ability to throw or to learn to throw breaking and change-of-speed pitches. However, a youngster starting to pitch at Little League age should concentrate on the fast ball and how to control it before working on other pitches. Thus, we come down to checking the speed of the ball and control. If a boy has poor control, he should be checked to see whether he grips and releases every pitch the same way. Only by getting a consistency of motion, a consistency of gripping and releasing the ball, and a consistency of rotation on the ball will a player develop control.

If a pitching candidate has hands so small that he has difficulty in gripping the ball, it is probable that he will have trouble with control. For this

Spring Tryouts

reason the candidate with large hands is to be preferred, everything else being equal. Again, everything else being equal, the pitching candidate who has good agility and running speed is to be favored. The ability of a pitcher to field his position is a valuable asset, and many games are won by the "fifth infielder."

In summary, when choosing a pitcher, first look for the fast ball, then for control, and third for ability to field the position.

FIELDING

In testing the outfielders, toss the ball from second base to the fielders about 60 feet away to screen out the inexperienced and uncoordinated, thus avoiding the possibility of injuring boys who haven't acquired distance perception. Toss one ball directly to the fielder, one to the left, and one to the right. Later you can give the better boys a stiffer fielding workout.

If you have enough infield candidates, have one infield back up another to save time in retrieving balls which the boys fail to field. Don't hit the ball too hard. The object is to give the boys confidence while checking their agility, mobility, and fielding form—not to show how hard the fungo hitter can bat the ball. Hit two balls directly at the fielder playing at normal depth, one to his left, one to his right, and one dribbler for him to charge.

BATTING

The problem of testing hitters has been left for last since hitters won't be of much value to a team if they can't run and throw. However, once the managers and coaches have determined the running and throwing skills of the candidates, it is important to find out whether they can hit or whether they can learn to hit.

If a boy is afraid of a pitched ball, the odds are against his becoming a good hitter. The batter must keep his arms away from his body, his shoulders and hips level, and his eyes on the ball from the time the pitcher releases it. Also check to see that the boy has good wrist action. If the boy is a "sweep hitter" he will have trouble hitting with power. To be a power hitter, it is probable that he will combine all the desirable batting habits, but particularly those which involve the short stride which permits the quick and full hip pivot, the breaking of the wrists, and the follow-through with the bat. It is the proper utilizing of the body and mind which makes it possible for a Charley Neal, who weighs 155 pounds, to hit a 430-foot home run in a World Series.

Perhaps the best way to insure a fair test for batters in Little League is to secure the services of three or four 13- or 14-year-old pitchers who have pitched enough in Little League or similar programs in recent years to demonstrate that they have control. Have these boys alternate in pitching to the hitters, throwing at a little better than half-speed.

Let each batter take three swings and bunt twice. Bunting can be an important factor at all levels of baseball, but remember that most boys can be taught to bunt even though they may have trouble doing so in the tryouts.

Once you have learned something about the boy's ability to hit live pitching, the best way to measure his power is to have him hit for distance off a batting tee. You must furnish your own power off a tee, and tests with major league players show that the power hitters always hit the longest balls off the tee. Let each boy hit three balls off the tee. (This test will be valid only if players have had some experience in batting off a tee. Otherwise they may miss the ball completely.) Of the boys who look like the best hitters, those with the most power will have the most value to you.

EVALUATION

The Little League player agent should secure volunteers to help him conduct the drills so that the managers can spend their time judging the players and recording their performances on a chart to be used in bidding for the services of the boys. Managers should be sure to note the mental attitude of the boys. Everything else being equal, you want the boys with the most hustle and desire. Sometimes these attributes may even count more than measurable physical skills, and they can't be disregarded despite the importance of the physical attributes.

A rough outline to use in evaluating the players might be based on the following scale of maximum points:

	Points
Best runner	8
Best throw for distance	5
Best throwing accuracy	3
Batting skill and power	5
Bunting skill	2
Fielding skill	4
Hustle, learning ability, and general attitude	3
Maximum point score if player excelled in all departments	30

4

Building a Team

In building a team, the pioneers of modern baseball discovered patterns which are essential to success on the field. John McGraw always wanted strength down the middle when he managed championship teams for the New York Giants. He wanted topnotch defensive players in center field, at shortstop and second base, and behind the bat. In checking the strength of the Chicago White Sox, 1959 American League champions, you will find it in those positions—Landis in center field, Fox at second base, Aparicio at shortstop, and Lollar doing the catching.

In the top teams of recent years you will find the same pattern. As examples, take the Dodgers with Snider in center field, Reese at shortstop, Robinson at second base, and Campanella behind the bat; and the Yankees with Dickey catching, Rizzuto and Gordon as the second-base combination, and DiMaggio in center field.

Connie Mack concluded that pitching provided 70 per cent of the strength of a club and proved it by winning pennants for the Athletics with such stellar mounds men as Bob Grove, George Earnshaw, Ed Rommel, Chief Bender, Eddie Plank, and Jack Coombs.

Add to this Branch Rickey's conclusion that it takes five championship players plus pitching to win a pennant under normal circumstances and you have a formula for building a team. By championship players, Mr. Rickey means players who can run, throw, field, hit with power, and have a desire to play the game to the best of their ability.

INFIELDERS AND OUTFIELDERS. Starting from scratch as manager, coach, or captain of a squad of players, who do you want to be your shortstop? You want the player with the strongest arm if he has the other attributes required of an infielder. He should have good running speed and agility and quick hands. Since the shortstop gets more fielding chances than any other player, he should have "glue in his glove"; he should be such a sure fielder that he will rarely fumble the ball.

It is desirable to have a second baseman with strong forearms and wrists which permit him to make quick snap throws. He must be able to get rid of the ball in a hurry without throwing with a big sweeping motion of the arm. The second baseman also has a wide territory to cover and should have good running speed, agility, and good hands.

Particularly in Little League and other junior baseball it is helpful to have a tall first baseman because beginners often make throws which aren't true to the mark. Of course, it is essential that he have flexible hands which do not fumble balls thrown to him. Agility also is desirable since a good first baseman should be able to leap for high throws, dig low throws out of the dirt, and leave the base to spear wide throws.

A strong arm is important to a third baseman. Balls are hit so hard in his direction that he can frequently knock them down with his glove and still throw out the runner. In fact, some players have gained a reputation for blocking the ball with their bodies, retrieving it and retiring the runner. Observers would comment about Pepper Martin, the St. Louis Cardinals' star: "He'll be a great third baseman as long as his chest holds out."

The catcher should be rugged but still have good enough mobility to field bunts and foul flies and to back up the bases. He should be able to throw quickly and with power and have leadership qualifications since he directs the play on the field.

In the outfield, the player with the best range should be assigned to center field. He directs traffic in the outfield and in most instances has the right-of-way to catch every ball he can reach. He should have a strong and accurate arm.

If there is a difference in the strength and accuracy of throwing arms of the other fielders, the one with the weakest arm should play left field. A weaker arm can be tolerated there because the throw is much shorter to third base from left field than from right field, and one of the key defensive plays in baseball is to keep base-runners on first base from going to third on hits to the outfield. Thus, a strong arm in right field is very valuable because players like Carl Furillo, Rocky Colavito, Mel Ott, and Al Kaline can throw out many runners advancing from first to third on singles hit to right field.

In amateur baseball it is not always possible to have enough skillful players to fill all the positions. Some managers and coaches use the same kind of tactics Paul Richards has used with success in the major leagues—shifting a good outfielder with a strong arm from right to left field if the batter is a right-handed pull hitter who is very likely to hit to left field in a crucial situation, and then switching the fielders back to their normal positions against a batter who hits more often to right field or sprays his hits to all fields. However, you can go overboard in your strategy and make so many shifts that you confuse your players or break down their confidence.

Building a Team

PITCHING REQUIREMENTS. As to pitchers, it is assumed that every manager wants a player who can throw with speed and control. But speed isn't enough. He should have a "live" fast ball. If a fast ball doesn't spin rapidly enough to "blur" as it approaches the batter, it is the kind of pitch good hitters like to hit. Add to the strong arm the ability to learn to throw other kinds of pitches, enough agility to be able to field his position, and the intelligence to study the batters and figure out their weaknesses, and you have a potential pitching star.

Not all successful pitchers have been able to throw with unusual speed, but those who lack strong arms must possess exceptional aptitude for throwing "freak" pitches. Examples are Hoyt Wilhelm with the knuckle ball, Carl Hubbell with the screwball, and Sal Maglie and Eddie Lopat with their variety of curves.

If you have a player who throws the ball with great velocity, yet fails to make the grade at some position, don't give up on him as a player until you have given him an opportunity to pitch. Some of the finest pitchers in baseball have started at other positions. Bob Lemon, Bucky Walters, and Sol Rogovan all started as third-basemen, but failed to make the grade because of low batting averages. Each became a major league pitcher, and Lemon and Walters were key factors in their teams' winning pennants. Rocky Colavito and Carl Furillo proved that they could pitch in the majors, but their managers believed they were more valuable playing every day in right field. Hal Jeffcoat did switch from the outfield to pitching with the Chicago Cubs.

Likewise, managers have shifted outstanding pitchers to other positions to take advantage of their batting ability every day. Ed Barrow did it with Babe Ruth after Ruth had been a winning pitcher in World Series play, and Branch Rickey did it with George Sisler after Sisler had proved that he could pitch on a par with Walter Johnson. Both became all-time stars at their new positions.

SPEED AND VERSATILITY. While it is true that every manager looks for good hitters and that no player except a pitcher can expect to advance far in the game without being able to hit close to .300, we often overlook the other attributes of excellent players.

For instance, how many people have commented on the great running speed of the Brooklyn Dodgers' infield when it comprised Billy Cox at third base, Peewee Reese at shortstop, Jackie Robinson at second base, and Gil Hodges at first base? Cox, Reese, and Robinson were outstanding runners, and in his prime Hodges was almost as fast despite his size. Even Roy Campanella, the catcher, ran with deceptive speed. In their prime, Campanella and Yogi Berra were very quick starters and could run the bases as fast as most infielders and outfielders.

As to arms, Cox, Reese, Hodges, and Campanella had great arms and sure hands, and Robinson had a quick arm and could make snap throws required of a second baseman. All the Dodger infielders could shift to other positions and play them with skill, and Hodges also was a first-rate catcher and outfielder.

On the subject of outfielders, the Dodgers of the late 1940's probably had the greatest collection of arms ever seen in one outfield with Carl Furillo, Duke Snider, and Andy Pafko doing the throwing. All three could cover enough ground to be acceptable center fielders, too.

If you have the privilege of working with players of that kind of ability, you won't have many problems.

5

Running and Sliding

Few baseball players realize the importance of running or of improving their ability to run in the over-all development of playing skills. While the player bats on offense and fields and throws on defense, he runs on both offense and defense. Branch Rickey always stressed speed in building his great teams because running ability is the most valuable asset a player can bring to baseball.

The ability to run fast makes it possible to beat out slow rollers in the infield, to take extra bases on long hits, and to steal bases. In the field, running speed helps the player to get in front of more ground balls and to go farther to catch fly balls. Most of the great players in the game have been very fast on their feet—men like George Sisler, Ty Cobb, Honus Wagner, Joe DiMaggio, Stan Musial, Phil Rizzuto, Willie Mays, Mickey Mantle, and Jackie Robinson.

A SPRINTING GAME

The longest run a player will make in a Little League game is 80 yards, and the longest in adult baseball is 120 yards—the distance around the bases. Since baseball is a sprinting game, boys should learn to run the way sprinters do.

Very few young players have been exposed to track training, and it is unlikely that any youngster is born with perfect running form. Thus, running drills will be beneficial to every boy. Moreover, it would be a good idea for every athlete to learn from the best available source as much as he can about running; in most cases this source is the nearest track coach.

Here are some tips which may be helpful. Most boys do not have long enough strides, but they can be taught to lengthen them. When moving at top speed, good runners generally have strides which exceed their height. For instance, a player who is 5'6" tall will have a stride longer than 5'6".

Nevertheless, a runner can also slow down by overstriding. The stride should be a comfortable one and one which brings maximum speed. The length of the stride depends on the runner's body build and the length of his legs. Ray Welsh, conditioning director for the Pittsburgh Pirates, has proved that the speed of players at all stages of development from rookies to 35-year-old veterans can be improved if the players have a desire to improve. Over a period of two years, Welsh increased the stride of Bob Skinner by nearly one foot, thereby helping him to become one of the best base-runners in the game.

Welsh's procedure in lengthening stride is to have the player start with his usual stride, if it is too short, and then to mark off lines for the runner to land on in practice, increasing the length of these lines about three inches at a time until the runner is striding at what should be a normal distance for him to get the best results.

As Welsh points out, it takes an adult from 15 to 18 steps to reach first base from the batter's box. If one adds one-half inch to each stride, that will add up to at least seven and one-half inches over the distance. How often are players thrown out by five or six inches in a season? At least 10 times in a short schedule such as is played in Little League and similar junior programs. Being safe those 10 times will add 10 to 20 points to a batting average and will be the difference between victory and defeat in many close games.

RUN STRAIGHT AHEAD. Every player must find the right stride for his physical makeup. It is equally important to point the toes so that one runs straight ahead. Welsh discovered that this will help players gain another half inch with each step, a total of seven and one-half inches between home and first. Players can practice by striding down a base line so that their feet come down beside the line, left foot on the left side and right foot on the right side. Many runners will find that they will have to point their toes in slightly as they run in order to stride straight ahead.

A runner should streamline himself as much as possible with all arm and leg action forward and backward, not sideways, and the movement in a straight line. He should run on the balls of his feet to have the proper bounce, spring, and balance.

SPRINTING. Quick starts are all-important in sprinting. Anyone who has seen Jackie Robinson steal a base will realize what an asset a fast start can be in baseball. However, there is a difference between starting to run in a baseball game and starting to sprint in a track meet.

The first stride on offense is out of the batter's box. After hitting the ball, the first step toward first base is with the foot nearest the catcher. Some players swing so hard that they are off balance and must straighten up and shuffle their feet to get into position to start running toward first. Outstand-

Running and Sliding

ing hitters like Ted Williams, swinging left-handed, and Rogers Hornsby and Joe DiMaggio, hitting right-handed, could take a good swing at the pitch and still be in balance to start running immediately.

Once in stride, the player digs in as a sprinter does in starting a race, gradually increasing his stride as he picks up speed. He should swing his arms straight forward and backward, the left arm going forward with the right leg, lift his knees high, lean forward, and take a long but comfortable stride. The athlete should maintain the "running angle" with head up, trunk leaning forward, and ankles, hips, shoulders, and head in line. A good arm swing helps to drive the runner forward.

One of the most common faults of major league players is that they watch where the ball goes after they hit it instead of beginning to run immediately. How often have you seen a boy bat a ball and then stop to admire his handiwork before heading for first? To get the best results, players should stride toward first base the moment the bat meets the ball and should depend on the first-base coach to tell them whether to try for an extra base.

In running between home and first base and between third base and home plate, a runner should swing out slightly to be sure that he is running in foul territory. In the last half of the distance between home and first, a runner should run on the outside of the base line in foul territory. Otherwise, he can be called out if the umpire feels that the runner interferes with the fielder in taking the throw at first base or in attempting to field a batted ball. Running in foul territory between third and home, the runner eliminates the possibility of being put out by being hit by a batted ball.

MAKE SHARP TURNS. Turning the bases takes practice, and every player

FIG. 3. Bill Virdon of the Pittsburgh Pirates shows excellent form as he leans in and makes a sharp turn in rounding first base during spring training.

should spend time at it. Every step saved can be the difference between being safe or out at the next base.

A player should make as sharp a turn as possible in rounding the bases. Regardless of which foot touches the base, he must be sure to hit the inside corner of the base and push hard in the direction of the next base. He should lean in toward the pitcher with his body like an airplane dipping a wing in making a turn, lowering his left shoulder. If his left foot contacts the bases, swinging his right arm toward the next base will help him make a sharp turn.

FIG. 4. Runner makes sharp turn at first base, hitting inside corner of base with foot, and leaning toward pitcher. He keeps eyes on the base to be sure he touches it.

Once he discovers that the ball has been hit into the outfield, he should take a big turn at first, daring the outfielders to throw him out. Some of the best runners will advance a third of the distance to second base. Then if an outfielder juggles the ball, hesitates in deciding where to make his throw, or makes an error, the runner can take an extra base or two. Jackie Robinson always kept pressure on the outfielders in this way.

In Little League play breaking from a base is different from baseball at higher levels since the player must be in contact with the base until the pitch reaches the batter. Thus the player will be facing the pitcher as he starts to run. He will use the same body action as an adult player who has taken a lead off the base, pivoting on his right foot toward the next base, striding with his left foot, and swinging the left arm in the same direction to help pull his body around and give him the desired fast break. The arm action is similar to that of an uppercut punch in boxing. He starts from a standing crouch with knees bent and back bent forward, the arms hanging loosely beside the knees.

Running and Sliding

HOW TO TAG UP. When tagging up at a base, in an effort to advance after the catch of a fly ball, the runner should lean forward and keep his eyes on the ball. As the ball is caught, he should push hard against the side of the base with his rear foot to get a good start. Most right-handers push off with the right foot and left-handers with the left foot.

JUDGMENT IS IMPORTANT. Judgment is an important factor in being a successful base-runner. The runner must develop the ability to judge distance, to detect at a glance whether the fielder is in a position to throw, and to keep in mind the speed, strength, and accuracy of the fielder. He must learn how to make use of his coaches and must know the skills of all the defensive players who may be involved in relays, cut-offs, or making the tag.

In baseball at older age-levels, base-stealing becomes important. A running club can and does upset the opposition. With a Willie Mays or Luis Aparicio on base, the pitcher can't concentrate fully on the batter because he must be sure to hold the runner close to his base. The catcher will be hesitant about signaling for a curve ball or change-of-pace pitch because breaking pitches and slow pitches make it more difficult for him to throw out a runner. Even though the curve, slider, or change-up may be the pitch the batter doesn't like, the catcher may call for a chest-high fast ball, which the batter is more likely to hit, because he can catch and throw it more quickly. A dangerous runner also causes pitchers to "waste" more pitches with the catcher calling for pitch-outs in an effort to pick a runner off base or to throw him out when he attempts to steal. Every time a pitcher throws a "ball," he helps the opposition, and every time he throws a strike he helps his team, so a pitch-out which fails to retire a runner always helps the team at bat.

Each player must determine for himself how far to lead off a base. This will depend on his reaction time, reflexes, and experience. A good rule for a beginner is to take a lead twice the distance of his height. He would lead off 10 feet if he is five feet tall and would increase or decrease the lead as he discovers his capabilities and potentialities. The lead will vary according to the opposing pitchers, too. Runners stay closer to first base when a left-hander is pitching.

In leading off, young players would be wise to use the "two-way" lead, taking the same body position as they do in Little League, but being prepared to break back to the base they have occupied if the pitcher attempts a pick-off or to break for the next base if he pitches to the batter. The body weight is kept equally balanced on both feet so that the pitcher won't catch the runner leaning in one direction or the other as he makes his throw. In going back to a base, he pivots on the left foot and takes his first stride with his right foot, using the opposite body action of that described in breaking for the next base.

Some of the outstanding professional base-runners evolve more complicated ways of taking a lead, but the "two-way" lead is much better for beginners.

A good base-runner must get the "jump" on the pitcher. He must study the pitcher's moves and mannerisms and break for the next base at the split-second he knows the ball is going to the plate. It was Max Carey, one of the great base-runners of all time, who said: "It isn't so much how fast you run as how fast you start running." Jackie Robinson would study the pitcher's feet because the feet reveal where the pitcher will throw before any other part of the body. Willie Mays claims that watching a pitcher's head helps him most, and Richie Ashburn checks the whole body of the pitcher for tips as to where and when he will throw.

While Max Carey would sneak off the base an extra half step when he planned to steal to get an extra edge on the pitcher and catcher, Peewee Reese would take a bigger lead when he wasn't going to steal because he didn't want to tip off his plans. However, both had perfect timing and seemed to be going at full speed by their second stride.

If a pitcher knows that a runner will make no attempt to steal, he can concentrate on the batter. The runner who makes false starts causes the pitcher to divide his attention and decrease his effectiveness. When a runner at first fakes a dash to second, he may cause the opposing catcher to call for a pitchout. This will help his teammate at bat by putting the pitcher behind the batter in the ball-and-strike count.

BE ADVENTURESOME. Remember that a runner must be adventuresome to be effective. You must take chances to steal bases. Only steal when stealing will help your team, not when you are behind 12 to 0 in the sixth inning. It is the calculated risk which gets results. Even a slow runner can steal a base if he knows his opponents. Jimmy Wilson came out of retirement to catch in a World Series when injuries had put younger catchers on the bench. He hurt both legs, but continued to play. When he got on base, Wilson noticed that the opposing pitcher and catcher were paying no attention to him, so he surprised everyone in the park by promptly hobbling down to second for a stolen base.

Any coach or player would profit by memorizing Ray Welsh's rules for base-runners:

RULES FOR RUNNERS

1. Develop an aggressive base-running attitude.
2. Run out every play.
3. Judge distance and position of fielders.
4. Know the quality of catcher's and fielders' arms.
5. Learn to get a big lead.

Running and Sliding

6. Study the pitcher's moves and personal mannerisms.
7. Get a reputation as a good base-runner. Help the batter behind you.
8. Be adventuresome—take a lead—draw the throw.
9. Alertness, aggressiveness, and desire to steal are important to a good base-runner.
10. Know where the ball is every moment.
11. Keep pressing for every advantage.
12. Take off at full speed.
13. Know the situation, the score, the count on the batter, the outs in the inning, the strong and weak throwing arms of the opposing fielders, and be willing to take a chance.
14. Run in a straight line.
15. Make your turn at each base, ready to start for the next on balls hit to the outfield.
16. When you drop your bat at home plate and head for first, resolve to circle the bases as quickly as is possible.
17. Touch all bases.
18. Keep in mind the tactical situation at all times.
19. Run out all hits—let the coaches tell you if the ball is foul.
20. Watch the pitchers while on the bench to learn their motions and system.
21. Pivot properly when running bases to reduce the distance that must be traveled.
22. Always slide when in doubt, and once you start to slide don't change your mind.

BASE-RUNNING DRILL

You can use the whole squad at once on a base-running drill. With a pitcher and catcher in their regular positions, place one runner on first base and the rest of the players behind him, an arm's length from each other, with their left feet on the foul line. The pitcher throws the ball to the catcher. As the ball reaches home plate, the base-runners all break toward second base, running in parallel lines. They pivot toward second with the right foot and take a full first stride with the left foot, swinging the left arm toward second as they stride to get a good start.

To add interest to this drill, one of the coaches can stand about 30 feet back of second base in line with third base and pick a winner as the players sprint from first base. You can work with smaller groups, too, and might use a stop watch to time them and check them for improvement from week to week. The players can trot back to first base and repeat the drill several times.

SLIDING

Because Little Leaguers are close to the ground, they are at the ideal age to teach sliding. If your players practice sliding every time they come to the park-either on high grass or in a sliding pit-it won't take long for them to learn how to slide, and thus to avoid the leg and arm injuries which result so often from improper sliding.

Use a cart or low platform on wheels to show boys how to assume the proper sliding position. Wheel them in to a base and show them what to do in the process of sliding. The first thing to teach a boy about sliding is that he is to land on his buttocks—where he has the most natural padding—with his arms and legs off the ground.

THE HOOK SLIDE. Since a player should learn to slide away from the ball to avoid being tagged, teach him how to hook slide. Many players make the mistake of sliding past the base before the hooking foot contacts it, thus giving the fielder more time to make the tag.

FIG. 5(a). The Dodgers use a "grease monkey" cart like the one pictured here in teaching rookies how to slide. They can be shown proper leg action as they are wheeled into a base. Here the player has right knee slightly bent as his foot contacts base, sliding away from the throw.

In sliding to the right, which should be done if the ball is coming from the left, the player should land on his buttocks with his legs turned sideways to the right. The right leg is stretched out to the right and off the ground, and the left leg points toward the base with the knee slightly bent so that the left foot will contact the base at the earliest possible moment and remain in contact with the base as the knee bends and the body slides on past the base. The player should keep his eyes on the base and the fielder who is attempting to tag him, and should keep his arms from hitting the ground as he slides.

Running and Sliding

FIG. 5(b). The foot remains against "outer third" of base as knee bends and body slides forward. Player keeps eyes on base and fielder who is attempting to tag him. His arms are folded against the body and are off the ground to prevent injury. The other foot is carried off the ground for the same reason.

FIG. 6. This runner has good action as he slides to the right, with slightly bent left leg contacting bag. He has landed where he has the most natural padding and gets extra protection from sliding pads. Many runners bend leg too far, giving fielder more time to tag them before they reach base. Helmet protects head from possible wild throw.

Be sure the boys don't jump in the air, but stay as low to the ground as possible when going into a slide. As they land, only the buttocks should touch the ground.

In hooking to the left, the player lands with his feet turned sideways to the left, with arms off the ground, and using the same hooking action as with the right leg.

THE BENT-LEG SLIDE. The bent-leg slide is a good one to use when going into the base on a force play. There is no tag to avoid and this slide is faster because it takes the player straight to the base.

As he takes off, he bends the right leg under the left, with the foot pointed sideways. He extends the left leg directly toward the base, keeping the knee slightly bent and heel off the ground. The force of his body as it slides into the base, plus an upward push by the right leg and hands, gets him off fast toward the next base in case of a bad throw or fumble.

FIG. 7. When there is a force-out situation and the baserunner doesn't have to avoid a tag, the stand-up slide is desirable. The left leg is extended toward the base, with the knee slightly bent, and the right leg is bent sideways under the left leg and held high enough so that it won't dig into the ground and cause an injury. The arms are held in the air also to prevent injury. As slider reaches base, he pushes up with right leg and hand to be ready to run again in case of a wild throw.

AVOIDING A BLOCK. If the ball beats the player to the bag and the baseman has the base blocked, he should slide past the base and slap it with his hand. This slide is especially effective at home plate.

HEAD-FIRST SLIDE. The head-first slide is dangerous, but can be used when the defensive team attempts a pick-off play. Diving back to the side of the base away from the throw and contacting it with an outstretched hand is the quickest way to get there.

Running and Sliding

WHEN TO SLIDE. The players should know that they can run faster than they can slide. Therefore they should run across first base, where they are permitted to run past the base, and across home plate, too, unless a slide will enable them to avoid a tag. The slide is necessary on a close play at second or third base because the player must keep in contact with the base. He can't run to the base and stop as quickly as he can slide into it. In approaching second or third base, the runner should slide if there is any doubt in his mind about whether a slide is necessary. At home plate, he should slide only if he sees that the ball has reached the plate ahead of him.

FIG. 8. This base-runner did the proper thing in running hard, using a normal stride, as he attempted to beat out an infield tap. Note his leg action as he comes down on the base and continues to speed straight ahead. Also note action of first-base coach in signaling for him to run hard "through" the base and not to make a turn since the play would be close at first.

6

Batting and Bunting

IN THE BEGINNING, BUNT!

To most players, batting is the most enjoyable part of baseball if they are able to hit with some degree of regularity. It is no fun to bat if you strike out every time. A player should enjoy batting if he can be taught to meet the ball with his bat frequently. A boy who hits a two-bouncer to the pitcher and is thrown out at first can always believe that he would have had a base hit if the ball had gone two feet to one side or the other of the fielder.

How does a player learn to meet the ball? The answer for most beginners would be to teach them to bunt. Any boy who can catch a ball should be able to bunt one. All he has to do is to catch the ball on the big end of the bat.

To help a boy to catch the ball with his bat, have him bring the bat back slightly as the ball contacts it (the catching motion). Most players find it easier to bunt if they square around facing the pitcher with knees bent and arms extended—but not straight or stiff—so that the bat is in fair territory at shoulder height. The upper hand on the bat handle slides almost up to the trade-mark. Many boys slide the hand up so far that they fail to cover the outside of home plate with the big end of the bat. A player must experiment with his grip and stance until he knows that he will be able to bunt any ball in the strike zone.

It is helpful to keep the defensive team from knowing when one is going to bunt. However, with beginners it is more important for the boy to be in proper position in time to control the bat and bunt the ball. Inexperienced bunters often move into bunting position as the pitcher releases the ball. Later they delay in assuming the bunting position as they learn how long it takes them to get ready to bunt.

FAKE BUNTS. Experienced players fake bunts occasionally to bring in the defensive players to protect against the bunt. The fake can cause a pitcher

Batting and Bunting

FIG. 9. Charlie Dressen shows a Little Leaguer how to slide hand up bat handle to bunt.

to throw pitches which are difficult to bunt (high fast balls) but easier to hit for most hitters than other pitches, provided they are in the strike zone. Or it can cause him to waste a pitch or throw a pitch-out if there is a runner on base and thus get behind the batter in the ball-and-strike count. And it can cause the infielders to play closer to home plate to protect against the bunt, making it easier for the batter to drive hits through the infield. Some of the top hitters, like Stan Musial, Pete Reiser, Alvin Dark, Mickey Mantle, and Duke Snider, have kept their opponents off balance with such tactics.

PASS UP HIGH PITCHES. In teaching bunting, emphasize that the boy must not bunt at balls above the strike zone. The one thing a player must avoid in making a sacrifice bunt is to pop the ball into the air because any ball bunted into the air can result in a double play.

If a player passes up high pitches, holds the bat at shoulder height, and bunts the top half of the ball, he should solve this problem. When he doesn't like the pitch, he should pull his bat back to keep the umpire from calling a strike.

The batter should aim to bunt the ball about five feet from the foul line and one-third of the distance from home plate to third or first base, depend-

FIG. 10(a). The batter is in a good relaxed position, with bat "quiet," arms away from the body, hands in front of the rear shoulder, legs in a normal spread, knees bent slightly, shoulders and hips level, and back foot against the rear line of the batter's box. (Note good position of the catcher, too.) Batter is preparing to bunt, but doesn't tip off the defense by moving into bunting position too soon.

FIG. 10(b). Batter pivots to face pitcher, sliding top hand (right hand for right-handed hitter) up the bat handle, moving bat in front of body into fair territory and holding it level, and bending knees for relaxed stance. He bunts "top half" of the ball to be sure it goes on the ground. He catches the ball with the big end of the bat, keeping eyes on the ball and body relaxed, but alert.

FIG. 10(c). Batter pulls bat back when he decides ball is too high to bunt, to avoid having a strike called against him.

Batting and Bunting

ing on where he wants the bunt to go. Place a piece of cloth at these two places during bunting practice to give the bunter a target. To control the direction of the bunt, the batter moves the bat handle so that the ball will rebound off the bat in the proper direction. He will learn this quickly with practice.

BUNTING FOR BASE HIT. There are two types of bunt for a base hit—the drag and the push. The right-handed batter's push bunt and left-hander's drag bunt are aimed about halfway between the first baseman and pitcher and just hard enough so that it is out of the pitcher's reach and forces the second baseman to move in so far to field the ball that he doesn't have time to throw to first base.

The left-hander's push bunt and the right-hander's drag bunt are aimed down the third-base line about one-third of the distance to the base and inside the base line about three feet. In executing each, the bunter starts to run as he meets the ball, but he must time the bunt so that he doesn't step out of the batter's box before he bunts the ball.

On the push bunt, the bat meets the ball in front of the body as the weight of the body shifts to the front foot and the bunter is striding toward first base with the rear foot.

FIG. 11. This action in the Little League World Series shows player attempting a push bunt for a base hit. He has shifted his weight to front foot, striding toward first base with rear foot as bat goes forward to meet ball. He must be sure to meet ball with bat before he strides out of the batter's box.

The bat is held at the side of the body in the drag bunt, and the foot action is approximately the same as in the push bunt.

Bunting for a base hit takes plenty of practice, but a boy with good running speed can keep the defense off balance by bunting occasionally. If the infielders are deep, he drops a bunt in front of them, and when the infielders move in he has a better chance to hit the ball past them or over them for base hits. The direction of the bunt depends on where the defensive players are stationed, how well they field and throw, and where the ball is pitched. An alert player will learn where and how to bunt according to the situation.

Many outstanding players use the bunt to break batting slumps, and some upset their opponents by faking a bunt and then hitting, or taking a swing at one pitch and then bunting the next ball that is pitched in the strike zone.

USE PLAYER'S SKILLS. Every manager should know the skills of his players, attempt to add to these skills, and make use of them. For instance, Jackie Robinson could bunt for a base hit as easily as he could lay down a sacrifice bunt. There was no percentage in having him sacrifice when he could advance a runner and beat out the bunt for a base hit.

In the 1959 World Series it was common knowledge among students of the game that Billy Goodman, the Chicago White Sox' third baseman, did not field bunts as well as most major leaguers. Likewise, a keen observer would have discovered quickly that Dick Donovan, the White Sox' pitcher, used a pitching motion which had him finish up facing the first-base line.

With such good bunters and runners as Wally Moon and Jim Gilliam batting left-handed and having trouble hitting Donovan, it seemed that a push bunt down the third-base line might be in order. Yet the only bunts attempted were drag bunts down the first-base line.

PRACTICE. While the use of the bunt in every branch of baseball can be a big asset, this is particularly true in the junior leagues. Many Little League coaches have proved that they can teach mediocre batters to bunt well. One coach in Montreal taught his lads to bunt so skillfully that they won high-level tournament games without any other offensive weapon.

The main reason players don't learn to bunt is that they don't practice bunting. A successful school coach solves the problem by putting a defensive team on the field and then having the batter attempt to bunt for a base hit. He makes his batters continue to bunt until they succeed in laying one down safely to move a runner on to the next base.

When the player has learned how to execute the sacrifice bunt properly, the coach has him begin to practice bunting for base hits. As soon as the player has learned to lay down the "sacrifice" bunt, the "drag," and the "push" bunt, he tries one of each whenever he takes his turn in batting

Batting and Bunting

practice. Each player must lay down a bunt properly before he is permitted to swing away.

BATTING FUNDAMENTALS

Before a boy can hit a ball there are at least two things he must learn:

1. Always keep his eyes on the ball. (Learning to bunt, batting off a tee, and standing beside a catcher as he warms up a pitcher can be very helpful here.)
2. Swing a bat he can control. (When in doubt, swing a light bat.)

FIG. 12. Here Jackie Robinson shows a Little Leaguer where to hold his bat as he gets ready to hit. Like Robinson, most batting stars hold their hands chest high in front of the rear shoulder, with arms far enough from the body to permit a good swing. The foot spread is usually about the width of the shoulders. They stand close enough to the plate to be sure to cover all of it with the big end of the bat.

THE STANCE. When the player steps into the batter's box, he should get as far back as he can, with his rear foot resting against the end of the batter's box. This will give him a longer time to look over each pitch before having to decide whether he should swing at it. At the same time, it forces the catcher to make longer throws to the bases and makes it more difficult for him to block or catch low pitches. The batter's feet should be

FIG. 13. To remind beginners to stand far enough back in the batter's box, place a cloth tape across the batter's boxes even with the rear end of home plate. Note the tape around the bat handle to remind batter to choke up an inch or two for better control of bat. This batter shows good body balance as he prepares to swing. The catcher should not attempt to catch from the "signal squat" because he cannot shift to catch wide pitches and to throw quickly.

FIG. 14. Here a right-hander who has a wider than usual foot spread is shown ready to hit. His stance also indicates good body control and balance. The catcher has good body position.

Batting and Bunting

spread at a comfortable distance. The wider he stands, the less likely he is to over stride, and he should make every effort to guard against over striding. He should check to see that his bat covers the width of home plate as he swings.

THE SWING. Teach the batter to keep his front arm away from his body and the bat back and quiet as the pitcher starts to throw. Most good hitters hold their hands chest high and in front of the rear shoulder and move the bat back (not up or down) from three to six inches as they begin to swing. They have a level swing and keep the hips and shoulders level, too. Many boys swing too hard and either miss the ball or fail to meet it squarely. If you have players who over swing, have them practice hitting to the opposite field in batting practice—right-handers hitting to right field and left-handers, to left field.

FIG. 15. The batter shows his head remaining in same position as bat goes forward. He pushes off rear foot and keeps level shoulders and hips throughout swing.

THE STRIDE. The only reason for a stride with the front foot is to turn it around so that the batter gets a hip pivot. He hits against a straight front leg and pushes with the ball of the back foot. This body action, coupled with a good wrist snap as he meets the ball, will add power to all drives. The shorter the stride, the longer he can follow the flight of the ball before committing himself. A study of outstanding batters shows that the length of their strides is from three to six inches.

FOLLOW THROUGH. Just as in throwing, the player must follow through with the bat for a complete swing after he hits the ball. His head should be pointed in the same direction at the finish of his swing as it is when the pitcher releases the ball.

USE A LIGHT BAT AND CHOKE IT. Few young players realize that the power hitters of baseball swing light bats. The lighter the bat, the faster the batter can swing it, and the speed of the swing puts the power into it. By using a light bat, a boy can also stop his swing before he breaks his wrists if he sees that the pitch won't be in the strike zone.

Charlie Neal, who amazed the spectators by blasting a 425-foot home run into the Chicago White Sox' bullpen in the 1959 World Series, swings a very light bat and grips it with his hands about two inches from the end of the handle. Even Ted Kluszewski, the most muscular slugger in the major leagues, discovered that switching to a lighter bat added distance to his blows. A check of the bat racks shows that Mickey Mantle swings the lightest bat for the Yankees and that Stan Musial uses the lightest bat for the Cardinals.

Only players who have no power and who like to punch hits over the infield prefer heavier and bigger-barreled bats.

TAPE THE HANDLE. Some boys feel that they are proving that they are strong by swinging the heaviest bat available and gripping it at the end of the bat. You might point out to these youngsters that it is easier to hit a nail with a lightweight hammer than with a sledge hammer and by gripping it an inch or two from the end of the handle. The same thing is true where ball and bat are concerned. Ty Cobb, the greatest hitter of all time, always choked his bat, and Al Rosen proved that you can choke up on the handle and still hit home runs. Put a piece of tape around each bat handle about two inches from the end to remind your boys to grip the bat above the tape for better balance and control.

To keep your boys from the temptation of swinging a bat which is too heavy, select light bats for your team. Only if you have a batter who is so strong that he pulls the fastest pitches foul, should you permit him to swing a bat of the maximum weight and size permissible in Little League or of a suitable weight in other leagues. Even then, to keep him from pulling foul balls, it might be more desirable to close his stance before giving him the heavy bat. (Have him move his front foot closer to home plate.) If the batter hits so late that he fouls pitches consistently to the opposite field (down the right-field foul line if a right-handed swinger), insist that he switch to a lighter bat and move his hands up on the handle.

BATTING DRILLS

Can players be taught to hit or are they born? Experts have various opinions, but there's little doubt that with good instruction and constructive drills a large majority of boys can improve as batters.

John Piurek established an outstanding record as a high school coach at West Haven, Connecticut, by concentrating on batting. For several years his assistant coach was a talented semi-pro pitcher who had played college baseball. He had good control and a variety of pitches, and his duty was to pitch batting practice every day. He would learn the weaknesses of the hitters and then pitch to those weaknesses. A boy was advised that he would see nothing but curve balls outside until he learned to hit them, if that happened to be his weakness. Players with normal aptitude will learn to hit most pitches if they see enough of them.

Of course, a player could concentrate so much on one pitch that, while learning to hit it, he might forget to hit others that he could hit before. This happened to Gil Hodges when he came up with the Dodgers. He saw nothing but curve balls in batting practice, and by the time he learned to hit the curve the opposing pitchers were getting him out on the fast ball. Then he had to learn to be ready for the fast ball, but still be able to wait for the curve.

Most amateur teams aren't as fortunate in having skilled batting practice pitchers available. But an enterprising manager or coach often can find an experienced pitcher in the community who might volunteer to do some pitching after work in the late afternoon, early evening, or on a Saturday to help the hitters.

EYES MUST FOLLOW BALL. One of the most common mistakes young batters make is taking their eyes off the ball too soon. While there's a common belief that good hitters follow the pitch till it meets the bat, this isn't possible. However, from the moment the pitcher begins his pitching motion, the eyes should follow the ball as far as they can. The head should remain quiet throughout the swing and should be pointed in the same direction at the finish as at the start.

Al Mamaux, in developing outstanding hitters at Seton Hall College, used a very effective drill. During the first week of practice, he required his batters to hit to the opposite field. Whenever a batter pulled the ball, he had to lay down his bat and chase the ball, losing his turn at bat. It was amazing how quickly this arrangement helped the hitters learn to hit to the opposite field.

This drill is very helpful in getting the batters to follow the ball. It is generally the boy who is trying to pull the pitch into the next county who also pulls his head around and loses sight of the ball when he swings.

Under normal conditions, there are two types of batting practice. First is the one in which it's desirable to have a pitcher with good control try to throw the ball at about 75% to 80% of his top speed while concentrating on getting the ball into the strike zone. This kind of pitching gives a batter a chance to warm up and get his timing under control. However, this kind of pitching alone will never develop a hitter.

As Branch Rickey has said several thousand times, a player likes to practice what he can do well. That is why a Tommy Brown could win the home-run championship during batting practice when the pitcher grooved fast balls where Tom liked to hit them. But he didn't get that kind of pitching once the game got under way. His time would have been much better spent working on his weakness at the plate.

Since players seldom will work on their weaknesses of their own volition, the coach must set up drills to help them. These drills should include "game condition" pitching, with the catcher giving signals and the pitcher trying to keep the batter from hitting the ball.

How you set up batting practice depends on the time available. The standard pregame pattern is a good one with each batter bunting twice before hitting away and then limiting his "hitting" to three swings. This should be a warm-up round.

The second round, when time is available, could be a "game condition" round with the batter limited to three strikes and the batting practice catcher calling the strikes. Whenever possible, work your batting-practice pitchers under simulated game conditions, too. Have one pitcher throw 15 pitches and then alternate with a second pitcher. This keeps the pitchers from tiring and gives them about an inning of action at a time. Luke Sewell used this pattern with very good results when he managed in the major leagues.

THE BATTING TEE. Every squad should have access to a batting tee. With the use of pressed wool or plastic balls, players can practice hitting against the side of a gymnasium, a basement wall, barn, or garage. If such balls are not available, baseballs can be hit into a net or against a backstop. Players can thus spend their spare time swinging a bat. Using this equipment they can even practice with some purpose during the winter months.

Ted Williams discovered the value of the tee when Bert Dunne was popularizing it in youth programs on the Pacific Coast. I brought it to the attention of Branch Rickey, who introduced the tee to the major leagues at the Vero Beach training base of the Dodgers, and it has become a standard training aid in most spring camps and professional parks.

In batting a ball off a tee, the boy learns where he must stand in the batter's box to protect the plate with the big end of the bat, where the ball should be met when he breaks his wrists, and the angle of the bat in hitting the ball to different fields. Mr. Rickey proved to several Dodger hitters the first year the tee was used that they couldn't cover home plate adequately from where they stood in the batter's box. This example should prove helpful to coaches whose boys like to stand even with, or in front of, the batter's box. The coach can also point out that hitters like Stan Musial, Mickey Mantle, Willie Mays, Hank Aaron, Nellie Fox, Gil Hodges, Harvey Kuenn, and Al Kaline stand as far away from the pitchers as possible.

Many boys stand too far forward because they begin playing ball on sandlots without using batting boxes and, consequently, get into the habit of

Batting and Bunting

standing beside the plate as they bat. Moreover, a few move up because they hear the "old wives' tale" that they can hit the curve before it breaks by moving forward. The only way this can be done is by moving forward about 60 feet, as curves begin to break when they leave the pitcher's hand.

But all the advantage goes to the batter who stands in the back of the box since he has a longer time to judge the pitch before committing himself; he won't be swinging at pitches before they reach the strike zone; and he'll force the catcher to catch more pitches outside the strike zone and to make longer throws to the bases.

FIG. 16. The batting tees helps to develop a full swing. This right-handed hitter has maintained good balance and kept head and eyes pointed at pitcher while pivoting body so that shoulders are reversed and bat behind his back at finish of swing.

The tee helps a player to keep his eyes on the ball, to take a full level swing and follow-through in furnishing his own power, and to take a short stride and stay in balance when swinging. I've seen major league players, using batting tees for the first time, break broom handles in attempting to swing at balls.

As to power, the tee is an absolute measure of power for a player who has had some experience in hitting off it. One spring at Vero Beach this was proved to the satisfaction of the Dodger coaching staff when Duke Snider, Roy Campanella, Gil Hodges, Carl Furillo, and Jackie Robinson showed the same power ratio off the tee as they did in collecting extra base hits during the National League season. Such knowledge can be helpful to the coach who wants to know the relative power of his players. Everything else being equal, he wants the long-ball hitter in the line-up.

A boy who learns to hit off a tee, with proper coaching, shouldn't acquire the bad habits which plague so many hitters—namely, the arm hitch, the overstride, and taking the eyes off the ball. Of course, a player must see live pitching in order to learn to time and follow the ball, particularly when the pitcher is throwing "breaking stuff" But the tee can be used in daily drills to help all young hitters, to give them familiarity with the bat and a pattern of good batting habits. A boy should not become a "sweep hitter" if he learns to hit off a tee.

HIT LINE DRIVES. In using the tee, the ball should be placed on a belt-high tee for the first drills. If the boy is hitting the ball properly, he should be hitting line drives without the bat coming into contact with the tee. He should be hitting the ball in the middle.

If he's hitting fly balls, in all probability he's lifting his front shoulder; and if he's hitting the ball on the ground he's lowering the front shoulder. His shoulders should be kept level in order to give him maximum efficiency with the bat.

Coaches should know that approximately seven out of ten line drives are base hits, while only two out of ten ground balls become hits and only one out of ten flies falls safely in the major leagues. Knowing this, Ted Kluszewski advised an audience of college coaches at a clinic that he attempts to hit line drives even though more flies become home runs. Ted says his high-fly home runs are "mistakes," and Stan Musial says the same thing.

Once a boy learns to hit belt-high line drives, the tee may be lowered to the knee level for practice in grooving swings at that height—the height which gives most batters the most trouble. Then raise the tee to the armpit height for practice at that level.

One boy who practiced all winter swinging at knee high and chest high balls by means of a batting tee found in the spring that he could hit pitches at those heights much better than the previous season, but that he was missing pitches over the middle of the plate. This prompted Fresco Thompson to comment that the boy shouldn't worry because Fresco suspected that the "fat" pitch was Yogi Berra's weakness, but nobody would groove a pitch to him or any other hitter to find out. Boys like to do what they can do well, and the tee can help them become better hitters.

AUTOMATIC PITCHER. While many teams and leagues can't afford an automatic pitching machine, it's a training device which also can prove very helpful, in bunting drills. If a coach has a batter who is a poor judge of the

Batting and Bunting

strike zone or who is afraid of pitches, the pitching machine can be especially helpful. When a batter sees more pitches, he gains confidence, and confidence is a great asset to a batter.

When no pitching machine is available, "fearful" hitters and wild swingers can be helped by having them take their batting stance near a home plate in the bull pen against a pitcher who is warming up. The batter must not swing at the ball, but should judge the pitch by calling "strike" or "ball" as it crosses the plate. The catcher can tell him whether he has judged it correctly.

IN THE BOX. While it is a good idea for young batters to get into the habit of swinging at good pitches because batters learn to hit by hitting, there are times when a batter should take the first pitch even if it is one he would like to hit. This would be the case when your team is behind by several runs, and one hit, even a home run, wouldn't gain much ground for you. The object is to tire the pitcher by having him make as many pitches as possible and to swing only when there are two strikes on the batter or when there are two or three runners on base.

It would be foolish to swing at the first pitch in a close game when the pitcher has walked two or three batters ahead of you. Yet this happened in a World Series game not many years ago, and the swinger popped up a high fly to the first baseman for an easy out.

Although it is true that most batters hit better when they are ahead of the pitcher in the ball-and-strike count, only two or three in all of the years baseball has been played have been able to build up good batting averages by being first-pitch hitters. One of these was Joe Moore, a fine outfielder for the New York Giants for many years. However, there have been hundreds of others who have handicapped themselves by being first-ball swingers. Once the pitchers learn that you like to swing at the first pitch they will aim the ball just outside the strike zone and you won't be swinging at good pitches. Once you begin to swing at such pitches, smart pitchers will keep throwing the ball a little farther off the plate and you'll be offering at balls you can't even reach to foul—let alone hit with the big end of the bat.

The greatest right-handed hitter of all time, Rogers Hornsby, believes that batters should "wait out" pitchers in the first inning and the last two innings of a game. In the first inning, a majority of pitchers have some trouble with control before they get "zeroed in on the target." In the late innings, many pitchers begin to tire. Fatigue affects their control and "stuff" so that taking a strike or two frequently causes pitchers to walk batters and the extra effort by the pitcher in having to throw more pitches is all in favor of the team at bat. A manager must know his batter and the opposing pitcher and instruct his players accordingly, but the foregoing is sound advice to follow in most situations.

7

The Batting Order

There are several theories about building a batting order. One school of thought believes that the generally accepted pattern is wrong. The theory of this group is that since a team should bring its best hitter to bat as frequently as possible, he should be the lead-off man. If you accept this theory, it would be logical to have your second best hitter bat second, third best hitter bat third, etc.

While this theory has some merit and should be kept in mind when planning your batting order, there are many things in favor of the generally accepted pattern. Take the batting order of the Chicago White Sox in the 1959 World Series as an excellent example of the logic which recommends the accepted pattern. Luis Aparicio, the lead-off man, had by far the best base-stealing record in the big leagues during the season. To have such a man in the lead-off spot gives a big lift to the following hitters. As Casey Stengel puts it: "I played a couple of years at Pittsburgh with Max Carey [one of the best base-runners in the history of the game], and he batted ahead of me. 'I will run on the first or second pitch if I get on base,' he would tell me. 'Oh, take your time,' I would tell him. 'There's no hurry.' Why shouldn't I say it? When Carey is on first base I know the pitcher isn't going to throw any fancy curves and knuckle's and spitters. I'm going to get that fast ball so the catcher gets a chance to make a good throw in case Carey runs. That's what the White Sox get [with Aparicio on base], and I got to hand it to them; they're smart."

LEAD-OFF MAN. He should be a good judge of the strike zone, a good "waiter" who seldom swings at the first pitch when the bases are empty. Frequently he is small in size and, being "hard to pitch to," often draws bases on balls. Ability to bunt for a base hit and running speed are big assets. Thus you can see why Al Lopez selected Luis Aparicio as his lead-off hitter.

The Batting Order

SECOND BATTER. If he is a left-handed hitter, this is a big plus. With the lead-off runner on first base, the first baseman holds him on base (in competition above Little League). This leaves more hitting room for a pull-hitter because, with the first baseman holding the runner at first, the second baseman has to cover most of the territory between first and second. Another asset of a left-handed hitter is that he partially blocks the view of the catcher, who must throw around him for a play at first and to a lesser extent in throwing to second base.

He doesn't need to be a long-ball hitter, but it is highly desirable that he be able to hit-and-run, with good control of the bat. Frequently he is a "choke" hitter, and he should be able to bunt since there are many situations in which the manager will want to use the "hit-and-run" or a bunt to advance the runner on base. Speed also is an asset. You can see Nellie Fox fitting into the pattern. He bats left-handed, chokes up several inches on the bat handle and punches hits through the "hole" between first and second base, has fine control of his bat, bunts well, and is a good runner.

THIRD BATTER. The third batter should be a good hitter, one who hits for extra bases. It is also helpful if he can run well to score on hits by the clean-up hitter. Jim Landis hit well for the White Sox, has excellent running speed, and drove in many important runs in key games. A little more power with the bat would make him an ideal "third hitter."

FOURTH BATTER. The clean-up hitter should hit the long ball and hit well with runners on base. With one or two of the first three hitters on base when he steps into the batter's box, his power can drive them home. Sherman Lollar was the "long ball" threat for Chicago throughout the season, hitting the most home runs and driving in the runners ahead of him as well as could be expected.

FIFTH BATTER. His qualifications are much the same as those of the clean-up man. Ability to hit the long ball should be the first consideration and consistency in hitting second. Ted Kluszewski, who came to the White Sox late in the season, provided the most power on the club, driving in runs with long "sacrifice flies" to the outfield and extra base hits and hitting consistently.

SIXTH BATTER. He is the second lead-off man since he frequently is the lead-off batter in the second, fourth, or fifth innings. It is very helpful if he is a good "clutch" hitter, too, because the batting ability of the hitters ahead of him in the batting order gives him unusual opportunities to drive in runs. Al Smith easily fits this description. He has speed and is a good clutch hitter, driving in runs far more frequently than might be expected from his batting average.

SEVENTH BATTER. His qualifications should be much like those of the second batter. Everything else being equal, the faster player should bat second and the slower runner seventh. Against right-handed pitchers, Lopez followed this pattern. Billy Goodman is a left-handed "choke" hitter who has good control of the bat and can hit behind the runner. However, he doesn't run as well as Fox. Against left-handed pitchers, Lopez replaced Goodman in the line-up with Bubba Phillips, who bats right-handed. Phillips runs very well and also has good control of the bat, spraying hits to all fields. This instance shows that it is not always possible to find batters on your squad who fit the classic pattern.

EIGHTH AND NINTH BATTERS. Normally the weakest hitters fill out the line-up, with the pitcher batting last in professional baseball. Not batting every day, he doesn't get a chance to sharpen up his batting eye and improve as much as players who bat regularly.

Many managers check the statistics to determine whether a certain batting order brings up hitters more frequently in certain situations. If a pitcher is a very good bunter, the manager might want to move him into the eighth position when he finds that the eighth-place hitter frequently comes to bat with none or one out and runners on the bases.

When the White Sox faced right-handed pitchers, Jim Rivera was in the line-up. His batting average was low, but his fine running speed and daring on the bases made him a third lead-off man, with the pitcher available to advance him with a bunt when necessary. McAnany, a right-handed hitter with a better average, batted eighth against left-handed pitchers and provided more of the consistency and power desirable in a second third-place hitter.

Lopez switched Kluszewski and Lollar, depending on left- and right-handed pitching, but the general pattern didn't change, and most managers agree that this method of building a batting order gets them the best results.

A word of caution to managers and coaches of junior teams—place the pitcher in the batting order according to ability. He may be one of your top batters. Don't scramble your offensive line-up from game to game. There is real value in letting your players learn what is expected of them in fulfilling definite assignments as batters. In other words, don't confuse them with too much strategy and high-powered thinking. Let them learn the offensive pattern and what batters should do according to their position in the batting order.

8

Infield Play

Baseball is played by teams and no team can succeed if the nine individual players fail to cooperate. Inevitably certain players will make outstanding plays during the course of a game or a season, but it is the ability of the athletes to play together which gets the best results.

Team play is particularly important in the infield. During his 60 years of major league baseball, Connie Mack observed that the great teams were those which combined ability with friendly relationships and team spirit. The players studied the strengths and weaknesses of their teammates and tried to compensate for them.

If one player couldn't cover quite as much territory as was expected of a major leaguer, the player next to him would move over a step to give him a lift. Practice helps a player learn what to expect of his neighbor in making the double play, relay, cut-off, and in many other situations which develop in a game. The players must learn to make split-second decisions as the plays occurs, but should think through the possible play situations which could develop as each hitter steps into the batter's box.

PREPARING TO FIELD. Many infielders handicap themselves by having their feet spread too far apart as the ball is pitched. They do not understand the value of having a low center of gravity and feet close enough together (about the width of the shoulders apart) so that they can break quickly in any direction in pursuit of the ball.

While it is true that the infielder should charge balls hit in front of him, the charge should be controlled. If he rushes in at top speed to field a "slow bouncer," it may take an unexpected bounce to one side and elude him. However, one can change direction more easily if he is moving forward at moderate speed.

In moving forward, the player should move with the body bent forward and hands close to the ground. He should take the advice of George

FIG. 17. Peewee Reese, one of the finest in-fielders of modern times before he became a Dodger coach and then a broadcaster, demonstrates to a Little Leaguer that he must keep his glove close enough to the ground so that the ball can't go under it.

Toporcer, one of the greatest coaches in the game, and always carry his hands lower than he believes the ball will bound. Ten times as many balls go under fielders' gloves as go over them.

Since the forward movement shouldn't be at top speed, the fielder should be prepared to make his quickest movements sideways. Peewee Reese, the Dodger shortstop, discovered during his playing days that having his toes pointed out at about a 45-degree angle helped him get a quicker jump on the ball hit to either side. Dodger infielders continue to follow Reese's pattern.

A very good routine for infielders—and outfielders—to follow in getting ready to field is the following:

1. Place hands on knees as pitcher is getting the signal from the catcher.
2. Drop hands in front of the knees with the face of the glove toward the batter as the pitcher begins his motion.
3. Hop forward two or three inches with the weight on the balls of the feet and fingers brushing the ground as the ball is pitched.

Another tip from Toporcer: "Don't follow the flight of the pitch. Focus your eyes on the batter. This will enable you to get a better jump on a

Infield Play

FIG. 18(a). Managers and coaches should teach their infielders (and outfielders, too) to follow this routine: As the pitcher is taking his signals from the catcher, the fielders should assume this position, with feet spread about the width of the shoulders, toes pointed out slightly, body in a crouch with the "tail" low, and hands on knees.

FIG. 18(b). As the pitcher begins his throwing motion, the fielders drop their hands in front of the knees, with the face of the glove toward the batter.

FIG. 18(c). As the ball leaves the pitcher's hand, the fielders hop forward on the balls of the feet and lower bodies so that the fingers of the glove touch the ground. This view shows heels off ground, with weight of body forward as player is ready to make a "cat-like" spring for the ball. He keeps his eyes on the batter.

batted or bunted ball. You can start to either side more quickly if you watch the actions of the batter during his swing, especially when a batter starts to bunt."

When Eddie Miller was the best defensive shortstop in baseball, they called him "The Crab" because he moved along the ground that way always crouched low. Honus Wagner, the greatest shortstop of all time, would tell young players that they weren't low enough if the backs of their gloves weren't dirty. Wagner used a glove as though it were a scoop shovel.

Few players can get rid of the ball with the speed of a Leo Durocher or Phil Rizzuto in their prime. The ball seemed to leave their hands the moment it reached their gloves. However, keep in mind that you can't throw a ball until you catch it. Some youngsters become over-anxious and try to throw the ball before they have control of it—with sad results. But don't delay the throw because every step a fielder takes before he throws is at least one step for the runner and probably more since the runner is moving at top speed.

Remember this rule: The player should be sure he has caught the ball and has his eyes on the target before he throws. Then he should throw as quickly as possible.

ADJUST TO CAPABILITY. Managers and coaches should help their players adjust to their limitations and capabilities. Like Peewee Reese, when he was an all-star shortstop, they should ask themselves: "Is the batter fast? Is he slow? Does he break fast from the plate? How much time have I to throw him out, because that will govern how far in I have to play him, or whether I can stay back near the grass and still nail him." If a fielder's arm isn't great, he'll have to play closer to the batter, and rely on greater agility to get balls to the right or left.

He'll have to think about the type of pitch that is being thrown and the hitting habits of the batter. Will he "pull" a slow curve if he hits it, or will he fail to get around on the fast ball? Does he hit through the box or down the line? How does he hit against this pitcher?

Plant in the players' minds that; they shouldn't be stationary fielders, but should shift with the hitters, weather conditions, and game situations. Keep them mentally awake as well as physically fit.

INFIELD FUNDAMENTALS

FIELDING GROUND BALLS. Teach young infielders to stay close to the ground, as shown in Figure 18. A large majority of errors are made because infielders let balls go under them. Point out to the boys that it is much easier to come up for a ball than to bend down for one at the last instant.

Tell them to move forward for every ground ball hit in their direction

Infield Play

unless it is hit so hard that they don't have a chance to move. To emphasize this, major league coaches often say, "Be sure to charge those line drives," just to keep the players thinking about going to meet the ball even though it may be impossible to do so. Boys must learn to play the ball and not to let the ball play them.

Instruct them to keep their nose pointed toward the ball and their eyes on it from the time it leaves the bat until they field it. Turning the head only gives the ball a better chance to hit the fielder in the face if the ball takes a bad hop. You can demonstrate this to your players by showing them how much narrower their faces are when they look straight ahead than when the head is turned sideways.

THROWING. Players should field as many balls as possible with both hands and grip the ball immediately with the throwing hand. In one continuous motion the hands and ball should be brought to the right side of the body if the player throws with his right hand and to the left side of the body if he throws with his left hand so that he can make his throw without any wasted motion. His throwing arm should be away from his body as he brings it back to throw.

Often, a boy doesn't have time to bring his arm back if he charges in to field a slow roller but must make a snap throw on the run. However, on hard-hit balls, he should push off his right foot and make an overhand throw. This is the same motion as an overhand pitcher's fast ball, with the ball spinning backward off the ends of the fingers.

MOVING SIDEWAYS. While it is highly desirable to field the ball in front of the body, there are times when fielders must move quickly to either side. The first step to the side should be with the foot farther from the ball, the player pivoting on the ball of the foot closest to the ball and stepping with the other foot as he moves to field it.

SHIFT WITH HITTERS. Impress on the players that they should think about the batter as he approaches the batter's box. They should know whether he is fast or slow to determine how much time they have to throw him out. They can play deeper on slow runners and batters who seldom bunt. If a player is both slow and a hard hitter, this will determine where the fielder should be. How hard the pitcher throws also is a factor, since batters are likely to hit late on fast-ball pitchers, and the fielders will shift accordingly. If you can get your boys to think about position play, you will do them a big favor.

Infielders often handicap themselves by playing too close to the batter. This is especially true of second basemen, who should be back at the edge of the grass in most situations. Urge your first basemen to shift with the situation, too. They should play deep unless there is a bunt situation.

FIG. 19(a). This second baseman awaits throw from catcher, with glove in front of left knee to remind catcher that throw should be aimed at that target.

FIG. 19(b). As he catches ball, he grips it with right hand, keeping glove around hand and ball.

FIG. 19(c). In the same motion he swings down to the left so that ball, gripped in both hands with glove toward runner, is between the base-runner and the base. Note position of his feet.

Infield Play

Point out that the fielder can get a better "jump" on the ball if he keeps his eyes on the batter once the ball leaves the pitcher's hand. He can learn from the batter's actions what he intends to do—bunt or hit—and sometimes in what direction.

TAGGING RUNNERS. To tag a base-runner, the baseman should straddle the base and face the runner. Then he should place his glove, with the ball in it, in the runner's path and let the runner tag himself out. The tag should be low so that the runner can't slide underneath the glove. The back of the glove should touch the runner, and whenever possible the ball should be gripped with both hands to keep the ball from being dislodged by impact with the runner. The moment the baseman tags the runner he should pull the ball away.

FORCE PLAYS. Players at all infield positions should use the same type of stretch the first baseman uses on force plays when the ball is being thrown to them. To shorten the throw they should step toward the ball with the left foot and gloved hand extended (assuming that they throw right-handed).

TARGET FOR THROWS. It is helpful to have your players give their teammates a target with their glove for throws. On force plays the target should be in front of the chest. Then if the throw is wild, the receiver can stretch in any direction to catch it in the shortest possible time. On a tag play, the glove should be in front of the knee closest to the base-runner.

TWO HANDS ON BUNTS. While there are rare instances when a professional third baseman who has large hands can scoop up a bunt with his bare hand and throw out the bunter, this play shouldn't be taught to Little Leaguers because their hands aren't large enough to grip the ball. Even the best of the pros rarely succeed in making this play. Instead boys should do as the professionals are taught to do—charge the ball and scoop it up with both hands and throw on the run with a snap throw.

DOUBLE-PLAY

THROW SHOULDER-HIGH. Emphasize that all throws to the pivot man should be shoulder-high so that he doesn't have to waste any time or motion in making the throw to first. The pivot man should hold his glove in front of his chest as he approaches the base to give the thrower a target.

The type of throw made by the fielder who starts the double play depends on where and how he fields the ball. It may be a side-arm, underhand, or overhand throw, but in every instance the ball should reach the pivot man at the shoulder-high level and be thrown so that it can be handled easily. The thrower should try to avoid shoveling the ball to the pivot man with both hands because it is harder to make an accurate throw this way and more difficult for the pivot man to pick up the flight of the ball. The pivot man should try to catch the ball with two hands so that his throwing hand is on the ball and able to grip it for an immediate throw. There is no substitute for practice in learning to handle the ball smoothly and rapidly on double plays around second base. Players must repeat these pivot procedures often to become proficient in manipulating them.

FIG. 20(a). As pivot man on the double play, the second baseman uses the "rock-back" method if the ball reaches him behind the base, touching the base with his left foot and pushing back out of the base line. He pivots on his right foot toward first base.

FIG. 20(b). He strides toward first base with his left foot as he throws. This "rocker" pivot was preferred by such famous second basemen as Billy Herman and Jackie Robinson.

ROCKER PIVOT. When the second baseman is the pivot man on double plays, he should learn two ways to make the play—the "rocker" and the "cross-over." If the ball reaches the second baseman before he gets to the base, it is preferable to use "the rocker." He simply rocks back from second base, touching the bag with his left foot and pushing back with it. At the same time he pivots on his right foot and steps toward first base with his left foot as he throws. This pivot gets him out of the base line to avoid hitting the base-runner with the throw and to keep the players from colliding as the runner slides into the base. (See Fig. 20.)

FIG. 21 (a). When the second baseman catches the ball over or in front of the base, he steps on the corner nearest first base with his left foot.

FIG. 21(b). He strides across the base so that he comes down on his right foot on the infield side of the base line and facing first base as he begins his throwing motion.

CROSS-OVER PIVOT. When the throw to the second baseman requires him to catch it on the run as he reaches the base, the "cross-over" is desirable. There are several ways to make the "cross-over," but long observation indicates that the best way for the boy of Little League age to do it is for him to step on the corner of the bag nearest first base with the left foot and stride across the base, making an effort to turn toward first base as he strides. As he lands on his right foot, he pushes off it and steps toward first base with his left foot as he throws. Again this action gets him out of the base line to avoid hitting the base-runner. (See Fig. 21.)

FIG. 22(a). When the throw is to the right of the shortstop, he steps on the corner of second base nearest the pitcher's mound with his left foot.

FIG. 22(b). He pushes off to the right to get clear of the base line as he strides toward first base bringing the ball back to a throwing position. His left foot will step toward first base as he throws.

SHORTSTOP INSIDE. When the shortstop is the pivot man, and the throw is on the inside of the base path, he should step on the corner of the base nearest the pitcher's mound with his left foot and push off the base to the inside as he strides past to get clear of the base line. As he lands on his right foot, he throws to first base, stepping toward first with the left foot as he throws. (See Fig. 22.)

Infield Play

FIG. 23(a). Many shortstops use the "drag" pivot when the throw is to their left side. In making this pivot, the shortstop strides to the outfield side of the base with his left foot and drags his right foot against the corner of the base as he catches the ball.

FIG. 23(b). When his right foot is past the bag, he pushes off it and strides toward first base with his left foot as he throws. This pivot also gets him out of the base path to make his throw.

SHORTSTOP OUTSIDE. There are several ways of contacting the base when the shortstop receives the throw on the outfield side of the bag. Perhaps the easiest way for a Little Leaguer to learn and use effectively is to step on the corner of the base nearest center field with the left foot—to stride across to the outfield side of the base line and pivot on his right foot as he lands and makes his throw, stepping toward first base with the left foot as he throws.

The pivot used most in professional baseball when the throw is to the outfield side of the base is for the shortstop to stride to the left of the base and toward first base with his left foot, dragging his right foot against the corner of the bag. When the right foot is past the base, he pushes off it and steps toward first base with his left foot as he throws. The drag is more difficult to learn, but, like the cross-step pivot, makes it easier for the shortstop to avoid a collision with the base-runner if the play is close. (See Fig. 23.)

FIG. 24(a). Here is the cross-over pivot made famous by Marty Marion when he was the all-star shortstop of the St. Louis; Cardinals. Taking a throw toward the outfield side of the diamond, the shortstop touches the corner of the base nearest center field with his left foot as the ball reaches his glove.

FIG. 24(b). His right foot swings behind his left foot in a cross step a:» he brings the ball back toward his right shoulder and grips it with his right hand to throw.

FIG. 24(c). He pushes off his right foot and steps toward first base with his left foot as he throws. The cross step to the outfield side of the base line takes him away from the path of the runner, who may be sliding into the base, and helps him to avoid hitting the base-runner with his throw. This is the fastest and safest outside pivot for shortstops.

Infield Play

SHORTSTOP CROSS OVER. Another pivot was made famous by Marty Marion of the St. Louis Cardinals when he was known as "Mr. Shortstop" in the major leagues. It is executed in the following way: Taking the throw on the outfield side of the diamond, the shortstop touches the centerfield corner of second base with his left foot; he swings his right foot behind and past his left foot in a cross step; and then he steps toward first base with his left foot. He throws as he steps toward first base, pushing off his right foot. The cross step enables the shortstop to get out of the path of the base-runner and make an unobstructed throw to first base. Most Little Leaguers can learn to perform this cross-over pivot without any difficulty at all. (See Fig. 24 on the facing page.)

STOPPING A DOUBLE STEAL. The catcher, the second baseman, and the shortstop signal each other if they expect a double steal with runners on first and third bases. The first baseman calls the play, shouting, "There he goes!" as the runner breaks from first base. The catcher is the key man. He must force the lead runner back by looking toward third base. If he has no play there, he must throw to second. The second baseman must take a quick look at the runner on third base, take a step or two to meet the throw from the catcher, and throw the ball back if the lead runner breaks for home. If the runner at third doesn't break, the second baseman steps back and makes the play on the runner from first.

The shortstop backs up second base. If the batter is left-handed, the shortstop may take the throw and let the second baseman back him up. The center fielder races in to back up second base in case a bad throw gets past the infielders.

RUN-DOWN PLAYS

When infielders have a base-runner trapped, they should try to chase him away from home plate. The player receiving the throw should give the thrower a target outside the base path to keep the ball from hitting the runner.

The important thing in a run-down play is to make the runner commit himself. Often a good fake throw with a full-arm motion and the faker taking his eyes off the runner and actually looking at the fielder who would receive the throw, will fool the runner sufficiently to make him change direction and run into the tag without a throw being necessary.

Once a runner starts in one direction, teach your infielders to narrow the distance between him and them as fast as possible. They should make the putout with a minimum of throws because each throw can produce an error. Speed in completing the play may keep other runners from advancing while the fielders are trapping the runner.

FIG. 25. In this run-down play, the fielder is making a good fake as he runs base-runner back to first. He made *a* complete swing with throwing arm toward first baseman, striding toward runner in same motion. This caused runner to reverse motion toward second so second baseman could tag him.

If the runner is standing still after the fielder has faked a throw, the fielder should run toward him and force him toward another defensive player. Then the ball should be tossed to the defensive player closest to the runner, giving him time to catch it and tag the runner.

Three players can practice this play to get used to making quick throws and tags. One will be the runner and the other two will try to trap him. They can alternate as defenders and runners to give each player practice in running, faking, tagging, and catching the ball.

Your players should never leave a base uncovered in a run-down play. To give you an example, the catcher and third baseman are making the run-down with the runner trapped between third base and home plate. The pitcher should cover home plate and the shortstop should cover third base with the left fielder backing up third.

CUT-OFF PLAYS

Being in the right position at the right time saves games and runs for the defensive team, and every effort should be made to keep runners from advancing another base.

THROWS TO HOME PLATE. If there is a runner on second base and the batter hits a single to left field, the third baseman is the cut-off man. He catches the ball only if the catcher shouts that there is no play at home plate.

When the third baseman cuts off the throw, it's probable that his throw will be to second base because the batter may be attempting to take second on the throw-in from left field. However, there are times when the batter takes a big turn around first without going on to second and a throw to the first baseman will catch the runner off base. The third baseman should line up for the cut-off so that he will be on a line between the thrower and home plate and about 10 feet on the home plate side of the pitcher's mound.

If the batter singles to right field or center field with a runner on second, the first baseman becomes the cut-off man. He lines up between the outfielder and the catcher about 10 feet on the home plate side of the pitcher's mound. The outfielder should throw the ball so that it will reach the cut-off man at head-height. Then it is easy for him to duck the throw and let it go on to home plate if the catcher shouts "Let it go!" Otherwise he can cut it off and throw to second or first base if there is a chance to make a putout on the batter.

THROWS TO THIRD BASE. With a runner on first base and a single hit to right or center field, the shortstop is the cut-off man, lining up between third base and the outfielder. The outfielder should throw the ball so that the shortstop can cut it off or let it go as instructed by the shouts of the third baseman.

FIRST BASE

The first thing to teach a first baseman is how to stretch from the base to "shorten" the throw to him. He should learn to step toward the thrown ball, with his right foot on the base if he is a right-handed thrower and his left foot on the base if he is a left-handed thrower. He can stretch farther this way, whether the ball is thrown to his left or right or directly at him.

As the first baseman strides to meet the throw, he should push back with the toe of his other foot against the side of the base to be sure that he is in contact with the base as he catches the ball. With beginners, it is a good idea to practice tossing the ball to them until they learn to do this properly.

Right-handed first basemen should turn in toward the infield as they throw to other bases, striding toward the base to which the throw is being made with the left foot, as they throw. They should not turn their backs to the infield as they pivot to throw, but should turn so that they can see what is happening as they prepare to make a play. Thus, they can change the play if something unexpected happens such as a base-runner falling down, and their throws will be more accurate if they keep their eyes on the target.

First basemen should leave the base to spear wild throws and then try to beat the runner to the base. They should give the catcher or pitcher a

FIG. 26(a). A left-handed first baseman gives the other fielders a target for a throw to first, with left foot on corner of base closest to thrower. Position of glove is reminder that chest-high throw is easiest to handle in "force outs."

FIG. 26(b). As he determines flight of ball, he steps forward to meet it and "shorten the throw." With practice first baseman can stretch several feet toward ball and increase the number of outs on close plays. He catches throws above the belt with glove up.

FIG. 26(c). Stretching toward outfield for wide throw, the first baseman pushes against corner of base with ball of foot. As a left-handed thrower he can stretch farther with left foot against base and right foot stretching forward with right arm. Note position of glove.

FIG. 26(d). Here he backhands a wide throw to the home-plate side of the base. Again note position of glove. First basemen can always stretch farther by turning bodies sideways and catching one-handed.

target by stretching into fair territory on bunts in front of home plate. On throws to second base, they should throw to the left or right of the base—depending on whether they field the ball in back of or in front of the base line—to avoid hitting the base-runner.

9

Outfield Play

Some young players and some not-so-young have the idea that outfielders can take a vacation while watching their teammates perform during much of the time involved in playing most games. Although it is true that outfielders seldom get involved in as much action as most infielders, Lefty Gomez was close to the truth when he stated that he owed his success to good physical condition and "a fast outfield."

Even one fast outfielder who has a strong desire to be involved in the game can make a difference in its result. An example was the all-star high school game in Torrington, Connecticut, in which Jim Piersall was playing center field for the Connecticut team. The ball was hit to the shortstop, who made an overthrow to first base. Piersall had charged in to back up the shortstop in case the ball got through him, but reversed his direction as the ball was fielded and thrown. He kept on running as the right fielder remained rooted to the ground as an observer, and it was Piersall who retrieved the wild throw as the ball rebounded off the fence, whirled, and threw a strike to third base to retire the runner.

In addition to backing up the infielders, there are times when an outfielder can help his team by racing in to cover a base on a run-down play or even by "sneaking" in on a pre-arranged play to take a throw on a pick-off play.

ADJUST TO THE SITUATION. Great outfielders like Piersall, Joe DiMaggio, Willie Mays, Jim Landis, and Al Kaline check the wind every inning, glancing at flags, tossing grass into the air, wetting a finger, or using other methods to help them judge how far and in what direction a ball will travel.

Their action isn't all physical either. Thinking about the game situation and what to expect of an opponent is most helpful to the player and his team. If he is a good observer, he can discover where the batter is likely to hit the ball, how fast he can run, and whether he can be expected to take chances;

Outfield Play 69

and by keeping in mind the score and the inning of play he will be able to anticipate the strategy of the opposing team.

An excellent example of observation occurred in a Little League tournament game at Goshen, New York, several years ago when the center fielder for Kingston noted that the clean-up hitter for the other team was a hard hitter and a slow runner. Thus, when this hitter hammered a hard grounder to center field, the outfielder threw him out at first base. This also required alert play on the part of the first baseman.

Observation and execution entered the picture in a game which decided the championship of the National League. It was the ninth inning. Cal Abrams, a good runner, was at second base and Duke Snider was the batter. Richie Ashburn realized that an extra base hit by the powerful Snider would win the game and that a long single would get the same results with Abrams on second. Under the circumstances the best strategy would be for Ashburn to play closer to the infield and for the Philadelphia shortstop to keep Abrams from taking a big lead.

Snider blasted a low line drive over second base, and the Dodger coach at third assumed that the speedy Abrams could score as the ball was sure to hit the ground before reaching Ashburn, who didn't have a strong throwing arm. However, the power with which Snider hit the ball, the short lead by Abrams, and Ashburn's shallow position enabled Richie to charge the ball, field it on the first bounce, and make an accurate and instantaneous throw to catch Abrams by several feet at home plate. This preplanning permitted the Phillies to win the pennant on Dick Sisler's home run in the tenth inning.

There will be days with a Carl Erskine setting a strike-out record in the major league World Series, or with an Art Deras doing the same in a Little League World Series, when the outfielders won't have much of an opportunity to participate in the defensive action. But this is no reason for the fielders to lose interest or to "loaf on the job."

Just to watch Enos Slaughter run off and on to the diamond is to feel the pep he puts into the game and the lift that he gives to his teammates. There are outfielders who compete with their teammates to see who can reach the dugout first after the third out of the inning. This keeps them alert, speeds up play, and helps them to stay physically fit.

Outfielders can participate in the game vocally, too. In a national high school tournament in Japan the center fielder for a Tokyo team sounded like a tobacco auctioneer as he kept up a steady stream of chatter to encourage his teammates. The remarkable thing about his cheering was the fact that he was shouting as loudly and enthusiastically with his team behind 8 to 1 in the ninth inning as he was when the first pitch was delivered.

OUTFIELD FUNDAMENTALS

Outfielders should be poised on the balls of their feet, with the toes pointed slightly outward, ready to move in any direction as the ball is pitched. They should keep their bodies low and arms loose to get a quick jump on the ball.

FIG. 27. Harvey Kuenn, outfielder for the Tigers and Indians, assumes "ready" position which makes it possible for him to move quickly in any direction to field a batted ball. He keeps his body low and bent forward, with weight on the balls of the feet, arms relaxed, and hands low. Feet are close enough together to give him quick movement sideways.

CATCHING FLIES. They should try to get under fly balls at the earliest possible time. Then they may have a chance to catch the ball if they have misjudged the distance or if the wind blows it in a different direction. If they are playing the "sun" field, they must learn how to shade their eyes with the glove if they don't wear sun glasses.

They should attempt to catch fly balls chest high. This gets them into position to throw instantly, and if the ball is juggled they still might be able to trap it against the body before it touches the ground. The basket catch has been popularized by Willie Mays, but most major leaguers catch fly balls with the fingers of the glove up and palm toward the batter when they have time to get set for the catch.

THROWING. All outfield throws should be made with the overhand motion and backspin on the ball. As the fielder catches the ball, he should step with the foot of his throwing hand and push off it to throw, stepping in

Outfield Play

the direction he is throwing with the opposite foot as he releases the ball. The throwing hand should grasp the ball as soon as possible after the ball reaches the glove, and both hands should be moving toward the throwing position to speed the throwing process.

He should be sure to follow through with his whole body as he throws. To be sure that he has followed through properly, he should bend his back and touch the ground with his throwing hand as he completes his throwing motion.

TRAFFIC CONTROL. The center fielder has the right-of-way on all balls he can catch, but to avoid collisions, he should call for the ball. He should shout "I've got it" several times and even wave his arms if he has time and the noise of the crowd might keep a teammate from hearing him. When one fielder calls for the ball, the fielder nearest him should back up the play in case of an error or misjudgment.

Even though the center fielder has the right of way in the outfield, there are times when another fielder will be in a better position to make the throw after a catch. For instance, the ball is hit about halfway between the center and right fielder with a base-runner in position to advance to third base. Probably the right fielder would be in a better position to field the ball and make the throw to the third baseman. Fielders should decide in advance who will make the play depending on their respective skills and the game situation.

GROUND BALLS. When the game is close and a run may score on a base hit to the outfield, the outfielder must field ground balls on the run the way infielders do. However, when there is little chance of making a putout with a quick throw and the fielder wants to make sure that the grounder doesn't get past him for extra bases, he should be taught to drop down on one knee to block the ball. He drops down on the right knee if he throws right-handed, catches the ball, springs up, pushing off with the right foot and striding with the left foot as he throws. He drops to the left knee if he is left-handed and uses the opposite foot and leg action.

Some outfielders prefer to make the "safety first" play on ground balls by keeping the feet close together and crouching to "surround the ball" with the body.

POSITION PLAY. Most outfielders play too deep. While it is true that it is easier to catch a fly ball in front of you than one behind you, players will find by checking that about ten balls fall in front of fielders for every one that they might have caught by playing farther from home plate. They can always move back when a power hitter comes to the plate.

LEARNING HOW. Since it is difficult for youngsters to learn the distance a ball will travel when hit by a batter, start out in the spring by tossing fly

72 How to Play Little League Baseball

FIG. 28(a). Since this right-handed outfielder has plenty of time to get under a high fly, he times his catch so that he is striding forward with his right foot as he catches the ball. He keeps his glove up and eyes on the ball until it is in the glove. A left-handed thrower would try to catch the ball as he strides forward with left foot. This action puts him in throwing position in quickest possible time.

FIG. 28(b). He completes the catch and his throwing hand moves up to grasp the ball as his glove brings it down.

FIG. 28(c). He pivots his body into throwing position as he grips the ball . . .

Outfield Play

FIG. 28(d). ...and hops forward on right foot to put more power behind his throw.

FIG. 28(e). He pushes off on his right foot as he throws with overhand motion...

FIG. 28(f). ...and brings arm forward with good elbow and wrist snap.

FIG. 28(g). Note position of right shoulder and arm as he completes follow-through to get maximum power behind his throw.

balls to your fielders. When they get to the point where they can catch those to the side and in front of them regularly, toss balls so they will have to field them over their left shoulders and then over their right shoulders while running away from you. Then begin to bat fly balls to them from home plate.

On balls hit over him, teach each boy to pivot on the foot farther from the ball and take his first step with the foot closer to it. If the ball is hit directly behind him, he should make his turn to the left if the wind is blowing from the right, and to the right if the wind is blowing from the left, because the wind will blow the ball in that direction. He should try to keep his eyes on the ball as he turns and runs to make the catch.

Also give your fielders practice in fielding balls which rebound off the outfield fence by throwing balls against the fence so that they can field them, whirl, and throw the ball to second, third, or home base.

Norman Larker's skill in retrieving balls hit against the left-field screen in the Los Angeles Coliseum was an important factor in the Dodgers' triumph over the Chicago White Sox in the 1959 World Series. It took hours of practice, but this practice paid dividends on such plays as the one he made in fielding Luis Aparicio's drive off the fence and in a continuous motion, pivoting and throwing so that Jim Gilliam could cut off the throw and snap the ball to Charlie Neal in time to put out Aparicio at second base, thus snuffing out a rally. By comparison with most major league outfielders, Larker possessed inferior talents, but constant practice enabled him to make the most of his ability and to become a valuable member of a championship team.

BACKING UP THE INFIELD. Outfielders should be reminded frequently to back up the play on every ball thrown or hit to the infielders and bases in front of them (left fielder should back up third base, the third baseman, and shortstop; center fielder should back up the shortstop, second baseman, and second base; and right fielder should back up the second baseman, first baseman, and first base).

WHERE TO THROW. Each fielder should know where and how to throw the ball, too. With the third baseman lining up as cut-off man on throws from left field to home plate, the fielder should aim his throw for the third baseman's head. On throws from right and center fields to third base, the shortstop is cut-off man, and throws should be aimed at his head. However, fielders with strong arms should be taught to throw the ball on the fly to the base, if the tying or winning run has a chance to score. The ball will get there faster traveling all the way in the air.

Young fielders should be shown that balls lose speed if thrown too high in the air. The lower the ball travels without touching the ground, the faster

Outfield Play

it will arrive at its destination. The ball should never be thrown at higher than a 45-degree arc and generally not that high at Little League distances. Finally, outfielders should be alert. Have them "talk it up" with words of encouragement to their pitcher and reminders of the game situation—how many outs, where the ball should be thrown if hit to them on the ground or in the air, etc. While the pitcher is taking his warm-up tosses and the first baseman is tossing grounders to the other infielders, have your outfielders throw fly balls to each other.

DRILLS

Among the most helpful special drills are those duplicating play situations, in which runners are placed on various bases, the fielders told the score and number of outs, and then the ball is batted or thrown to them. This gives them a chance to make the proper play and to be corrected if they fail to do so.

A very important drill for young players involves catching balls in the sun field. A boy never knows when he may be required to play the "sun field," so it is important for him to learn how to shade his eyes while following the ball.

All fielders can be placed in the sun field, with the coach tossing balls about 75 to 100 feet to them, with the players shielding the sun with the gloved hand and following the ball into the glove with the eyes. Later, balls can be batted from a longer distance as the boys learn to follow the ball.

It is a good idea for all outfielders to take turns fielding ground balls in the infield from time to time so that they will become familiar with the proper way to field grounders in the outfield.

10

Catching

The catcher should be the most intelligent player on the team because he has more decisions to make and is responsible for calling more plays on the field. Adding interest to his assignment is the fact that he is involved in more action than is any other player.

There are at least three physical requisites for success in catching—durability, agility, and hand speed. When you have observed the quick movements of a Yogi Berra in pouncing on two bunts in succession to throw out runners at third base in a World Series game with the Dodgers or the split-second starts of Roy Campanella in speeding after pop flies, you realize the value of rapid mobility in your catchers. Obviously it takes durability for a catcher to remain alert and aggressive in every inning of every game. And hand speed is especially valuable in catching foul tips and breaking pitches—knucklers, screwballs, and sharp-breaking curves.

GOOD CATCHING HABITS. The biggest problem to overcome in developing catchers is to get them to be ready to throw quickly and accurately. Too many catchers stay down in their "signal squat" to catch pitches. It is not easy to comprehend why this happens. One reason seems to be that photographers invariably pose catchers in that position for pictures. Youngsters see these pictures and surmise that this is the proper position for receiving the ball.

With some older players it becomes a lazy habit. When there are no runners on base, some major league catchers stay down in the "squat" position and some even catch on one knee. An alert batter has a good chance of dropping a bunt in front of home plate and beating it out for a base hit if he finds a catcher receiving in this position.

So few batters take advantage of the carelessness of a catcher that it is easier for him to become careless. Nevertheless, the catcher handicaps his team when he is not in the best possible position to break in any direction as the ball is pitched, catch a pop fly, retrieve a wild pitch, or field a topped ball which may bounce in front of the plate.

To show what can happen when a catcher gets careless, recall the situation in the 1959 World Series when Sherman Lollar, one of the best catchers in the game, signaled for a curve ball outside, shifted out, and dropped to one knee before Shaw released the ball. Shaw's pitch was inside and got past Lollar, permitting Dodger runners on first and second to advance a base. When Shaw charged up to the plate to discuss the play with Lollar, it was obvious that he thought Lollar should have caught the pitch. It is unlikely that he would have missed it if he had been in a proper position to catch the ball.

When a catcher moves to the inside or outside of the plate before the ball is pitched, he may tip off the opposition as to what kind of pitch to expect. Dropping to a knee generally indicates that he has signaled for a curve. But if a catcher gets into the habit of catching from the same (proper) position all the time, he avoids tipping off his strategy, and he has the freedom of movement to get in front of every pitch in the vicinity of the strike zone.

Branch Rickey has observed that a key factor in catching is the ability to get into a position to throw at the earliest possible moment. This means that the catcher should catch as many pitches as possible with the weight of the body on the right foot. In the few instances when this cannot be done, he should shift his weight to the right foot as soon as possible. Combining this action with bringing the ball up to a throwing position in a continuous motion as the ball is caught will keep the opposition from running wild on the bases.

The Chicago White Sox discovered this when Johnny Roseboro's good catching form, aggressiveness, alertness, and accurate arm combined to throttle their attack when they met in the World Series. His ability to throw instantaneously turned the base-running speed of the White Sox to the advantage of the Dodgers as he threw out runner after runner until the Sox quit running.

Early in his career Yogi Berra had so much difficulty in attempting to curb the running of the Brooklyn Dodgers that he was replaced by Aaron Robinson in a World Series. Only the expert instruction of Bill Dickey and hard work by Berra in learning to catch and throw in a continuous motion made it possible for Berra to make proper use of his strong arm and to develop into an outstanding catcher during the following season.

FINDING A CATCHER. Finding a catcher is usually the most difficult assignment in filling positions for a baseball team. This is not always because boys don't want to be catchers, but more often because boys have trouble in learning to play this position. Wearing more equipment, catching the ball which a batter is attempting to hit, avoiding batters in throwing to basemen, and other skills are requirements of catching that are not common to other positions.

Since these situations make it necessary for a catcher to spend more time in learning his position than is generally necessary for other players, Little League teams should make a practice of training one or two extra catchers each season. These boys should be among the younger players on the squad so that they will be eligible to catch in the league the following year. A good way to train the youngsters is to have them catch batting practice while wearing mask, chest protector, protective cup, and leg guards.

Keep in mind that catching requires more strength and endurance than other positions and urge rugged youngsters to try out for the position. Although there have been few left-handed catchers, there is no reason why a southpaw can't catch. A team from Texas had a talented left-handed battery in a recent Little League World Series.

There are some advantages to having a left-hander behind the plate. Normally it is easier for a left-handed catcher to catch breaking pitches from a right-handed pitcher, particularly when the batter is right-handed. He may have trouble in getting a catching mitt, but manufacturers will make mitts on order.

Catchers who wear glasses are becoming more common, too, both in professional and amateur leagues. However, be sure that your catcher has a mask which fits properly over his glasses if he wears them while catching. Finally, remember that it is highly desirable to have a lively or "peppy" catcher who will keep your other players alert and on their toes,

FUNDAMENTALS

The catcher is the quarterback of your team. He has the whole field in front of him and is the only player in a position to see whether or not the other players are in their proper places and ready for action. Thus, he should double-check before each pitch to see that his teammates are in position and should hold up play until they assume the proper position.

THE SIGNALS. Once the defense is properly aligned, the catcher assumes the "signal squat" with his right knee pointed toward the second baseman and left knee pointed toward the shortstop. His left forearm rests on his left thigh so that his mitt is in front of and against his knee, with the back of the mitt facing the third baseman. The signals are given with the right hand, the fingers resting against the base of the right thigh to keep anyone behind him from seeing the signs.

The system of signals becomes more complicated as you advance in baseball. The basic pattern is to call for a fast ball with one finger, curve with two fingers, a change of pace with three fingers, etc. If you think your foes

Catching

FIG. 29(a). Here the catcher gives signals to the pitcher, squatting so that his right knee is pointed toward the second baseman and left knee pointed toward the shortstop. His left forearm rests on his left thigh so that his mitt is in front of and against his knee, with the back of the mitt facing the third baseman. The signals are given with the right hand, the fingers resting against the base of the right thigh to keep anyone behind him or runners at first or third base from seeing the signs.

are picking up your signals, use a series of signs, such as: one finger, two fingers, one finger for the fast ball; two fingers, one finger, two fingers for the curve ball.

READY TO CATCH. After he gives the signals, the catcher stands up with his weight on the balls of his feet, and body bent forward. This must be emphasized to catchers because many of them try to catch from the "signal squat" and in so doing are unable to shift quickly to get in front of a wide pitch, jump to stop a high throw, move forward to field a bunt, shag a foul ball or back up third or first base. Insist that he keep from catching from the "lazy man's crouch."

FIG. 29(b). When he signals, the catcher stands and measures his distance from the batter before assuming his catching stance. With arm extended (right hand toward a left-handed batter and left hand toward a right-handed batter), the hand should be from six to twelve inches in back of the batter's hands and bat. This should keep the batter from coming into contact with the catcher when he swings the bat.

THE TARGET. Once he has assumed a comfortable stance with his feet spread apart slightly wider than the width of his shoulders and the left foot slightly ahead of the right foot (about three to six inches), he should give the pitcher a target with his mitt—the front of the mitt facing the pitcher—and hold it still until the pitcher throws the ball. A target between the belt and the knees—with the fingers of the mitt pointing toward the ground—is preferable most of the time because a large majority of batters can hit pitches between the shoulder and belt farther than they can hit low pitches.

The catcher should be sure he is centered behind home plate so that he gives the pitcher a good target by outlining the strike zone with his body. The pitcher should aim at some target on the catcher's body (left shoulder, right knee, bottom of chest protector or some other spot) to be indicated by the catcher when he gives his signals to the pitcher. The catcher should be an arm's length in back of the batter as he lines up to receive the pitch. To avoid being hit by the bat, he should not move forward to meet the ball until

Catching

FIG. 29(c). At the proper distance from the batter, the catcher assumes a comfortable stance with his feet spread slightly wider than the width of his shoulders. He is centered behind home plate, holding the glove down as a reminder to keep the pitches low unless the catcher has signaled for a high pitch. (Low pitches get the best results against most batters.) His throwing hand is relaxed and half-closed with the back of the hand toward the pitcher and close to the mitt so that it can cover the ball quickly.

after the batter swings. This is particularly important with beginners in the batter's box and behind the plate, as they often do the unexpected and injuries can be the result.

RELAX THROWING HAND. The throwing hand should be relaxed and half-closed as the ball approaches the mitt. It is desirable to have the back of the hand toward the pitcher because the joints of fingers and wrist will bend with the ball if they are hit by a foul tip, and the hand is in the proper position to reach into the mitt to grasp the ball and make a throw quickly. The throwing hand should be held close to the mitt.

SHIFT FOR PITCHES. On wide throws, the catcher steps toward the ball so that he can get in front of the pitch. With a right-hander at bat, and a pitch to the outside, he steps to the right with his right foot as he makes the catch. Then he steps in the direction he wants to throw with the left foot. On an inside pitch, he steps to the left with his left foot and moves the right foot slightly to the rear of the left foot as quickly as possible. Once again, he steps forward or in the direction he is throwing with his left foot as he throws.

When left-handers are hitting, he steps to the left to catch the outside pitch and to the right to catch the inside pitch. He catches pitches above the crotch with the mitt up and below it with the fingers of the mitt pointing down.

As the batter swings at the ball, the catcher's arms should move forward rapidly. In case of a foul tip, this will give him a better chance to catch it before it changes direction too much. The body should go forward with the arms in sort of a "rocking chair" motion until he starts to catch the ball.

THROWING TO BASES. Once the ball reaches the mitt, the catcher should bring his arms back toward his right shoulder so that he can use the overarm motion with an elbow and wrist snap to get a backspin on the ball for

FIG. 30. The catcher should shift into a throwing position the moment he receives every pitch as this catcher has done. He should attempt to catch each pitch in front of his body, not to one side. He should step sideways to get in front of wide pitches.

better carry on all throws. He must learn that accuracy is more important than power.

A catcher who can grip the ball and release it quickly and accurately without taking an extra step or a big windup in throwing often gets more assists than a player with a stronger arm who takes a longer time to get rid of the ball and then tries to throw so hard that he sacrifices accuracy.

The catcher should aim his throws at the left knee of basemen who are preparing to tag runners trying to advance. If the baseman hasn't reached the bag, the throw should be aimed at the corner of the base to which the runner will be sliding and about one foot above it. If the runners are caught off base at first or second, the throw should be aimed at the right knee to let the baseman make the tag with a minimum of effort and a maximum of speed. Throws to first and third bases should be made inside the base lines to avoid hitting the runner and the basemen should stretch into the infield to give him a target for such throws. If a catcher's throws are short of their target, he should lengthen his stride in throwing. If his throws are too high, he should take a shorter stride as he throws.

BLOCK LOW PITCHES. A passed ball can cost your team a run. To make sure that a low pitch doesn't get past the catcher, he should drop to his knees, while keeping his head down, and smother the ball.

POP FLIES. In shagging a pop fly, he should notice where the ball has been hit and toss his mask in the opposite direction to avoid stumbling over it as Hank Gowdy once did in a World Series. He will find it easier to catch pop-ups with the face of his mitt up at about the height of his chest. He should get under the ball as fast as possible. Only frequent practice will enable him to judge the ball hit straight up, because it will spin toward the infield as it comes down. It is a good idea to let infielders catch fly balls hit about halfway between them and the catcher. It is easier for them to judge the flight of balls hit toward them.

TWO HANDS FOR BUNTS. The catcher should rush forward to handle bunts hit in front of home plate. If the ball is halfway between him and the pitcher or first baseman, he is in a better position to make a throw and to see where to throw the ball. He should stop bunts with his mitt, scoop them up with his bare hand and make a snap throw in what seems to be almost one continuous motion. Using both hands helps him to make the play with much less chance of bobbling the ball.

PLAYS AT HOME PLATE. If the catcher has time on plays at home plate and if the throw is accurate, he should catch the ball in front of the plate and turn so that he has the ball gripped in his mitt and bare hand—with the back of the mitt between the runner and the base—and brush tag the runner as he slides into the base. He should be sure he is low enough to keep the run-

FIG. 31. As he awaits the throw, the catcher should move out of the runner's path so as not to block the plate without possession of the ball. It is against the rules and could lead to injury. Runners should run across the plate, as demonstrated here, because they can run faster than they can slide. Slide only to avoid a tag at home plate.

FIG. 32. Here an alert catcher has made a forceout at home plate and immediately shifts into throwing position for possible play at third base.

ner from sliding under the tag. On throws from right field or the second-base side of the diamond, he should stand with home plate between his feet to take the throw. If the throw is from the left-field side of the diamond, he should be beside the front of home plate and facing the runner. He must tell the cut-off man (generally the first baseman on throws from right and center field, and the third baseman on throws from left field) to "Cut it off! Cut it off!" or "Let it go! Let it go!" depending on whether he has a chance to make a play on the runner.

FIG. 33. This catcher has moved out to get in front of low, wide throw. Note his good fielding position, with low center of gravity as he is prepared to pounce in any direction for ball if it takes a bad hop. The base-runner shouldn't jump into the air and throw up his hands because he slows his forward progress. He can move faster by maintaining his regular stride across home plate.

On force plays he should stretch for the throw like the first baseman does with his right foot on the front edge of home plate. The catcher has no right to be on the base line or home plate unless he has possession of the ball, and the runner is entitled to advance a base if he is blocked by a fielder who doesn't have the ball. Be on the safe side and keep your catcher off the third-base line.

BACK UP FIRST. When there are no base-runners in scoring position, the catcher should get in the habit of racing into foul territory behind first base

FIG. 34. Here a catcher in Little League World Series directs play on the field, holding up hands to show that there is no chance to get the runner at home plate.

to protect against overthrows on throws to first base. When a runner is on first base and the ball is bunted to the third baseman, the catcher should cover third base.

HELP THE PITCHER. The catcher must know his pitcher and how to work with him. His throws back to the pitcher should be chest-high. He can slow up or speed up play, as seems desirable, by taking his time in returning the ball or snapping his throw back in a hurry. Unless the pitcher has exceptional control, he should encourage the pitcher to make every effort to get ahead of the batter in the ball-and-strike count before worrying about pitching to a batter's weakness.

It is important for the catcher to study the opposing hitters during their batting practice to discover what pitches they seem to like and what pitches they hit with the most power. Noticing where they stand in the batter's box, whether they crouch or stand up straight, whether they hold their arms away from their bodies, or whether they have a hitch in their swing will be helpful in deciding how to have his pitcher pitch to them.

As an example, it is common knowledge that most "hitch" hitters (those who move their bats down and up as the pitch is coming toward them) have trouble in hitting a good fast ball, but have good success hitting "change-up" pitches because the slower pitches give them time to level off their swings after the hitch.

If a batter moves around in the batter's box from pitch to pitch, the catcher can adjust for this movement, too.

CATCHING DRILLS. With beginners, it is a good idea to spend a few minutes each day in having the boys walk through the movements they will use in signaling, giving the target, shifting to the left and right, and throwing. Then balls can be tossed to the catcher to his right and to his left to give him practice in shifting. The catcher should wear all of his equipment in practice to simulate an actual game situation.

During batting practice, he can be instructed to throw to the bases, throwing to first base if the first batter misses a pitch, throwing to second base if the second batter misses a pitch, throwing to third base if the third batter misses a pitch, throwing to first base if the fourth batter misses a pitch, etc. If he throws more than one time during the batting turn of each hitter he will delay practice too much to make the drill practical.

Special drills should be set up for fielding fly balls, hit straight up from home plate. It is difficult to fungo such fly balls and amateur managers and coaches may have to stand beside the plate and throw such balls into the air even though they don't have the same spin as a ball hit into the air. Few catchers get enough practice in fielding foul flies despite the fact that this is the hardest play required of a catcher.

During play-situation drills, it is a good idea to let the catcher practice the defense against the double steal with runners on first and third bases. Roy Campanella always would glance at the man at third. If he was too far off third, he would throw there to pick him off. Otherwise, he would throw to second in an effort to catch the man coming from first. To be sure he will make an accurate throw, the catcher should be sure he is looking at his target before he throws.

Practicing the run-down play also pays dividends. A good fake often will trap the runner without a single throw. Mack Burk, while catching for Williamsport, tagged out a rival Eastern League catcher 15 feet from third base without releasing the ball after catching it at home plate. His opponent had taken a big turn at third base so Burk went through the motions of throwing to third, looking past the runner and striding and swinging his arm forward with a good simulated motion. He began to run toward third with his motion as the base-runner shifted his weight to head for home as he believed that Burk was throwing the ball. When the runner saw Burk coming toward him, he changed directions again, still watching Burk. Again Burk faked a throw in the same way and the base-runner again changed direction, making it simple for Burk to tag him.

This is the play Mr. Rickey taught his catchers at St. Louis, Brooklyn, and Pittsburgh, and it was so effective that Mr. Rickey could use it to trap Jackie Robinson in a practice drill one spring at the Dodgertown training base. Robinson was in his prime and Mr. Rickey about 70 years old at the time.

To teach the catcher to block pitches which bounce into the dirt in front of him, have your pitcher toss balls at half-speed so that they will land on or near home plate. When the catcher learns to smother or catch balls bounding directly in front of him, have the pitcher throw to either side of the plate to give the catcher practice in blocking wide pitches, too. In play-situation drills, the catcher should also be given an opportunity to tag runners at the plate, and back up throws at first and third base.

11

Pitching

What are the attributes of a good pitcher? Students of the game seem to agree that control comes first on the list. You can have a pitcher with "all of the stuff in the world," but his career will be brief if he fails to control it.

Normally, a pitcher can come to a consistency of pitching in a relatively short period of time. If he grips the ball the same way every time he throws it, and throws with the same motion, he should be able to throw to the same place with regularity. Then, if he is wild, his pitches will be wild in the same place, high and outside, or low and inside, and so forth. If this pattern develops, you can help the player by having him lengthen his stride to throw higher, or shorten it to throw lower; hold on to the ball longer to throw lower, or release it sooner to throw higher; change the direction of the striding foot to move the ball inside or outside; and using a different target.

Mr. Rickey once signed a young pitcher in the South who threw the ball "with all the speed the ball could stand." However, the boy never advanced higher than the bottom rung of the professional baseball ladder because his hands were so small that he couldn't get a good grip on the ball and thus was plagued by control trouble. From then on, Mr. Rickey always checked the hands of prospective pitchers to be sure that they were large enough to get a good grip on the ball.

The size of the body doesn't seem to be of primary importance to pitchers if they have good coordination. They can be tall and wiry as the Dean brothers, Lefty Gomez, and Preacher Roe were in their prime and as Don Drysdale and Jim Bunning are today, or built more like fullbacks along the lines of Allie Reynolds and Early Wynn, or on the small side as are Whitey Ford, Ed Lopat, and Bobby Shantz. However, large hands, strong wrists and forearms are very helpful to a pitcher.

One reason many young pitchers have trouble with control is that they try to be too careful with their pitches. Instead of aiming for the corners, they should concentrate on getting the ball over the plate against most hitters. If a boy can throw hard or has "good stuff," he need not worry about the batter getting many hits in a game. The percentages are with the pitcher. Once the pitcher gets ahead in the ball-and-strike count, the percentages increase in his favor. Major league statisticians have proved that batters don't hit as well when they are behind the pitcher. The farther behind batters get—for example, two strikes and no balls—the worse they hit. This shows why it is so important for the pitcher to get ahead in the count. Once there are two strikes on the batter, the pitcher can aim for the corners of the plate or try to miss the strike zone by two or three inches in an effort to make the batter chase a bad pitch. Of course, if a pitcher has very good control, he should pitch to spots consistently.

LOW PITCHES TAKE AWAY POWER. Probably the best control pitchers ever to appear in the Little League World Series were Joey Sims of Birmingham, Alabama, and Angel Macias of Monterrey, Mexico. Neither could throw with as much speed as some other mounds men who have appeared in the tournament; but their ability to throw the ball where they wanted it to go made them unbeatable.

Both kept their pitches low, thus taking away the power of opposing batters. Studies prove that the large majority of extra-base hits are produced by hitting pitches above the belt. Macias struck out a power hitter with three inside pitches the first time he faced him. When the batter moved away from the plate the second time at bat so as to be set for the inside pitch, Macias poured three straight strikes over the outside corner of the plate and struck him out again.

This episode brings to mind the conversation of two members of the Baseball Hall of Fame about how to pitch to batters. George Sisler asked Mordecai "Three-Finger" Brown about his style of pitching. Brown replied that he pitched high to batters who crouched over, pitched low to batters who stood straight up, pitched inside to batters who crowded the plate, and pitched outside to batters who stood away from the plate. If you don't know the weakness of a hitter, this is still a good pattern to follow.

CONTROL BALL AND TEMPER. Personal discipline is more important to a pitcher than to any other player. No matter what happens—adverse umpires' decisions, errors by his teammates, the actions of his opponents—the pitcher must keep his emotions under control if he is to remain effective on the pitching mound.

Effective pitching requires complete coordination of mind and body. An agitated mind will lose control of the body. How many times do you see a pitcher lose his temper because a decision goes against him or because an opponent hits a home run? Often enough for you to know that by the time he regains his composure and gets back to pitching in his normal pattern the game has been lost.

When teammates make errors, they are quick to blame themselves and will work harder for the pitcher who grins when the breaks are going against him. The pitcher who gives credit to his team when he wins and assumes his share of the blame when he loses is the pitcher who will gain the wholehearted support of his teammates.

Once a pitcher "blows his top" by sounding off at an umpire, teammate, or opponent, perhaps the best way of helping him discipline himself is to remove him from the game as soon as you can warm up a pitcher to replace him. His temperamental flare-up probably has destroyed his effectiveness as a pitcher for the day, and removing him from the game will serve as a lesson to him and other members of the team who may be tempted to lose their tempers.

LET UMPIRES MAKE THE DECISIONS. The parent or adult leader who permits the young player to blame his failures on the umpire can create the kind of incident that happened in the Eastern League some years ago when a promising rookie pitcher reported to Manager George Stirnweiss of the Binghamton club. The rookie did some of the greatest acting since Barrymore as he pantomimed his displeasure at any call of a borderline pitch which was not in his favor. One could sense from his portrayal that he wanted the spectators to realize that he was a fine, stalwart youth who was doing his best to get along in the world, but that the umpire was a blackhearted villain who was working against him.

Stirnweiss watched this performance for nearly two innings, and then he charged off the bench to the mound as though he were still carrying the football for the University of North Carolina. Obviously he was not impressed by the pitcher's histrionics, and later questioning brought out what he told the pitcher: "Young man, it is time that you make an election of professions. You can be an umpire, an actor, or a pitcher, but you can only be one at a time when you are playing for me. Right now it is your job to pitch. Leave the acting to the actors and umpiring to umpires or you won't do any more pitching here." The rookie followed Stirnweiss' sound advice; otherwise his baseball road would have been a rocky one.

FIRST FUNDAMENTALS

THE GRIP. A young pitcher must learn how to grip the ball before he throws it. He should hold it with the second and third fingers resting on a seam at the top and with the thumb directly underneath. It should be

FIG. 35. Carl Erskine, who holds the Major League record for strike-outs in a World Series game, shows a Little League pitcher how to grip the ball so that the thumb is directly underneath and the second and third fingers on top of the ball, with the ends of the fingers gripping seams so that they can make the ball spin rapidly when released. Erskine also emphasizes the importance of holding the ball upright so that the elbow and wrist can snap forward and down in throwing to make the fast ball spin backward in flight.

gripped so that four seams will spin in the air as it is thrown, giving the batter less white surface to see as well as more raised surface to provide friction to help the ball hop or break. As the pitcher throws, he should lead with his elbow, and snap the elbow and wrist forward to make the ball spin

Pitching

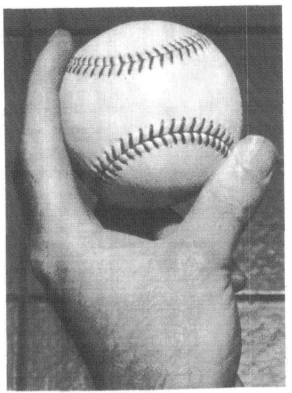

FIG. 36. Here the pitcher grips the ball with the ends of his fingers so that the four seams will spin in the air as it is thrown. This spin gives the batter less white surface to see and more raised surface of seams to provide friction, thus helping the ball "break."

 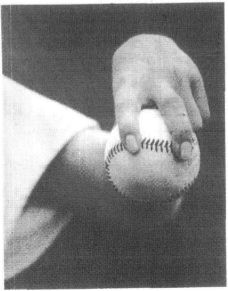

FIGS. 37(a), (b). These pictures show a pitcher practicing the wrist and hand action required in throwing the fast ball. All young players should get into the habit of flipping their throwing hand forward in this way.

FIG. 38(a). In taking signs from the catcher, the pitcher stands with the foot under his gloved hand (right foot if he is a left-handed thrower) behind the rubber, and foot under his throwing hand (left foot if he is a left-handed thrower) located so that the heel is on the rubber and ball of the foot in front of the rubber. He holds the ball behind his back.

FIG. 38(b). As he begins his motion, his arms swing upward, glove hiding ball from batter as he pivots to the left.

FIG. 38(c). Pivoting on his left **foot,** he swings his right knee past his left knee and his arms come down with the glove still covering the ball. His eyes remain on the target throughout the pitching motion.

Pitching

FIG. 38(d). As his right foot starts toward the plate, his left hand, gripping the ball, goes back toward second base. He pushes against the front of the rubber with his left foot to put power into the pitch.

FIG. 38(e). This side view shows how the body is turned sideways as the ball starts forward. Professional pitchers generally swing the glove forward at shoulder level to distract the batter's eyes from the ball.

FIG. 38(f). This picture shows the forward whip of the arm in throwing the fast ball and the stride straight toward the plate.

FIG. 38(g). As he follows through with his motion, the pitcher's arm swings past his opposite knee and his shoulder is pointed toward home plate.

FIG. 38(h). After completing his follow-through, he instantaneously hops into a crouch, swinging his glove in front of his chest to protect against a line drive. He faces the batter with weight on his toes so he can break in any direction for batted ball.

backward. The fast ball should roll off the ends of the fingers. The faster the ball spins the more life it will have and the more effective it will be. It is this elbow and wrist snap that makes the ball spin.

TAKING SIGNALS. In taking signs from the catcher, the pitcher should stand with the foot under his gloved hand (right foot if he is a left-handed thrower) behind the rubber, and the foot under his throwing hand (left foot if he is a left-handed thrower) located so that the heel is on the rubber and the ball of the foot in front of the rubber. The position of the feet is reversed if he is a right-handed thrower.

With runners on base he may want to straddle the rubber when getting the signal to avoid the possibility of balking. In this case he steps onto the pitching rubber before he starts to throw.

He holds the ball behind his back and covers it with his glove as he swings

Pitching

into action. Most pitchers prefer to wear large gloves—the better to hide the ball.

A stretching windup helps pitchers to keep their muscles loose and to get better body action. As they start their pitching motions, most pitchers bend forward and then rock backward with the glove hiding the ball from the batter.

THE PITCHING MOTION. As the arm swings upward, the pitcher turns the foot under his throwing hand so that he pushes off the front of the rubber with the side of his foot and gets more power behind his pitch. At the same time the knee of the other leg swings in front of the knee of the pitching foot as the body pivots sideways and the pitching arm swings backward toward second base. He steps directly toward home plate as he throws and follows through with his whole body.

It is helpful to swing the gloved hand high to help hide the ball and keep the batter from seeing it until it is actually released by the throwing hand. As his motion begins, the shoulder of his throwing hand should be pointed toward second base and as he finishes the motion, the shoulder of the throwing hand should be pointed in the direction of the catcher. This motion insures a complete body pivot and follow-through and takes strain off the shoulder.

When throwing to the batter, a pitcher often ends up off balance and in a bad position to field a batted ball. By taking a quick second step with the foot under the gloved hand, the pitcher can square around to face home plate. He should come up on the balls of his feet to get a fast start toward any ball hit in his direction and should bring up his glove in front of his chest to protect against line drives. A pitcher should throw with a quick, but smooth motion, making as few unnecessary movements as possible. He should not try to throw so hard that he cannot control his motions. Sometimes pitchers rear back too far, kick too high, and take too long a stride— and their control suffers accordingly.

You may recall how Herb Score's brilliant pitching career was sidetracked when a line drive off the bat of Gil McDougald hit one of his eyes. Score's pitching motion and follow-through were excellent, but he always ended up with his body facing third base and his glove behind his back.

Before the accident, Score could throw a ball at more than 100 miles an hour. McDougald swings a bat at 115 miles an hour. Dr. Creighton Hale calculated that this combination of speed propelled the ball back toward Score at more than 100 miles an hour. Knowing the normal reaction time of a major league player, Hale concluded that the ball would have traveled more than 45 feet before Score could determine its direction of flight. Meanwhile Score moved forward approximately six feet with his pitching motion, bringing the ball to within nine feet of him. Thus he had no chance to

FIG. 39. Many young pitchers don't get their bodies behind their pitches. Here a right-hander in Little League World Series displays an excellent follow-through as his body goes forward, the shoulder aimed at the plate and arm swinging past his left knee.

swing his glove around in front of him for protection because he had no time to react to the situation after determining his danger.

If Score had been taught to take a second step and hop into a crouching position, while swinging his glove in front of his chest the instant he had completed his follow-through, he should have avoided serious injury. Young players who want to see pitchers who execute this motion very well should watch Lew Burdette, Bobby Shantz, Larry Sherry, Johnny Podres, and Billy Loes on television.

CONTROL. A number of things can affect a pitcher's control. First on the list is taking his eyes off the target. From the time a pitcher begins his throwing motion, he should keep his eyes on the place he wants the ball to go until it reaches its destination. To perfect his control, the pitcher should aim at a target every time he throws. In warming up, he can pick out some spot on the catcher, such as his left knee, and throw at that spot until he

Pitching

FIG. 40. Here another Little League World Series pitcher shows proper follow-through for a left-hander as his shoulder and arm swing forward. Note how he keeps his eyes on the target, bends low and seems to "pour his body" into the pitch without any strain. Stiff-backed pitchers handicap themselves.

gets so that he can hit it. Then he can try the right knee, left shoulder and right shoulder.

Be sure that your pitcher grips the ball and releases it the same way every time he throws a particular type of pitch, such as a fast ball or change of pace. He should step in the same place each time he pitches, too. Otherwise, he probably will be a scatter pitcher who will have control trouble. If a boy grips and releases the ball the same way every time and is still wild, he should be wild in one particular place—such as high and outside. This you can correct by having him let go of the ball a little sooner or a little later as the case may be—sooner if he is throwing too low and later if he is throwing too high.

Slightly changing the direction of his stepping may help the pitcher to zero in on the target if he is pitching outside or inside consistently. If his pitches are to the left of the strike zone, have him stride a little farther to the right. If they are to the right of the plate, have him stride a bit farther to the left. Shortening the stride may help a pitcher who throws balls too high

FIG. 41. Joey Jay played on the first Little League team formed in the state of Connecticut and is the first athlete to enjoy participating in both the Little League World Series and Major League World Series. Here Jay displays fine pitching form as he strides directly toward home plate with his elbow leading and elbow and wrist beginning to snap forward to release fast ball off the ends of his fingers. He keeps his eyes on his target.

consistently, and lengthening the stride may help a pitcher who throws too low.

THE CHANGE OF PACE. When a pitcher has learned to throw the fast ball properly and to control it most of the time, he may want to experiment with another pitch. This may be the time to teach him a change of pace. To throw the fast ball properly, he should grip the ball with the ends of his fingers, leaving space between the ball and the crotch of the hand.

For the change of pace or "slow ball," the pitcher pushes the ball back against the crotch of his hand as he begins his pitching motion. His index

Pitching

FIG. 42. This grip is for the change of pace or "slow ball." The ball is pushed back into the crotch of the hand and the ends of the second and middle fingers are raised slightly as the ball is released. To throw the batter off in his timing, the rotation and motion should be the same as with the fast ball. However, this grip will slow up the flight of the ball. It often takes a long period of time to learn to control this pitch.

and middle fingers are on top and his thumb underneath the ball in approximately the same grip as for the fast ball. He lifts the fingers slightly as he releases the ball, keeping them relaxed and looser than for the fast ball, but throws both pitches with the same motion to fool the batter. If he uses the change of pace, impress upon him the importance of throwing it only to batters who are having success in hitting his fast ball. If a batter can't hit the fast ball, the change of pace may be just the pitch he can hit successfully.

BREAKING PITCHES. There are many ideas and theories about when and how pitchers should begin to throw curve balls. Research indicates that throwing curves puts more strain on the arm than throwing fast balls because the twisting motion is not a natural one. However, a young player's bones are less brittle than when he matures, and he has more elasticity in his arm.

It is true that there is a limit to the number of pitches any arm can throw without wearing out! Throwing curves hastens the wearing-out process, but the limit varies with each individual. Tom Sheehan, the scout and pitching coach for the San Francisco Giants, was striking out members of a threshing-crew in a game on his father's farm with a curve ball when he was 12 years of age. Thirty years later his curve was still good enough to fool hitters in professional baseball. Clarence Mitchell, who pitched the Brooklyn Dodgers into a World Series, could throw a sharp-breaking curve when he was 50 years old.

Probably the pitch which puts more stress and strain and "wear and tear" on the pitcher than any other is the screwball. Carl Hubbell used this pitch with outstanding success for many years.

Although these examples are unusual, they indicate that the curve ball doesn't have to be a dangerous pitch for a player to include in his repertoire if he knows how to throw it properly and if he refrains from using it too frequently. In fact, the evidence would indicate the real danger is that pitchers will injure their arms by trying to throw "trick" pitches without the benefit of proper coaching when their coaches refuse to show them how to throw curves, sliders, knucklers, and change-ups. Often pitchers will experiment by themselves if adults refuse to show them how to throw a certain pitch.

THE CURVE BALL. To throw a curve, the pitcher should be relaxed and hold the ball firmly, but not tightly, by the thumb and the second and third fingers, as shown in Figure 43. The grip should be fixed with the glove hiding the ball from the batter before the pitcher begins his pitching motion.

Almost all successful pitchers spin the ball off the second finger, snapping the wrist forward to give the ball a forward spin as it is released. Beginners should do what major league pitchers do each year as they begin spring training, tossing the ball at short distances and concentrating on getting a good spin on the ball and then gradually lengthening the distance they throw and increasing the speed with which they throw. For at least a week, boys should not throw the full distance.

The player should attempt to make the ball spin as rapidly as possible because it is the spin of the ball which makes it break. No youngster should try to throw a curve ball "hard," but should concentrate on throwing the slow curve and controlling it. He should keep in mind that it is not the speed of the pitch, but how fast he can spin the ball which is important.

Any player who doesn't have a stiff wrist should, with sufficient practice, be able to throw a curve. It may be that Little Leaguers should spin a few curves in practice for a full season before attempting to throw one in a game.

As in the case of the fast ball, the overhand curve is the best pitch for most pitchers. It is easier to control and will break downward, making most batters hit on top of it if they don't miss it completely. The overhand curve generally makes batters hit ground balls, cutting down the distance of hits and giving the infielders a better chance to field the ball. A sidearm curve, on the other hand, normally breaks sideways so that a batter can be fooled by it and still hit it solidly if he meets it in the strike zone.

It should be emphasized that the elbow leads the wrist and hand in the motion, with the elbow extended forward from the shoulder and the wrist snapping downward with the back of the hand toward home plate as the hand turns in releasing the ball. The second finger becomes the last contact with the ball, pressing against a seam to give it spin.

If the fingers grip the ball too tightly, the wrist will tighten up also, preventing a good wrist snap, and the extra tension may cause the arm to tire. Some pitchers find it easier to throw a good curve by shortening their stride slightly.

Pitching

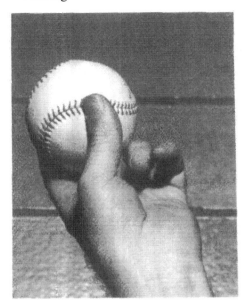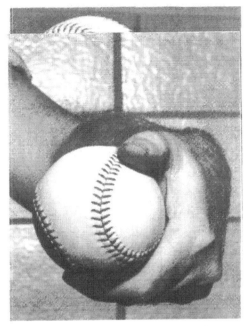

FIGS. 43(a), (b), (c). These photos show the hand and wrist action used in throwing an overhand curve, with the wrist rolling out and down as the ball spins off the ends of the fingers and over the top of the second finger. Beginners should go through this motion slowly as they start to use it.

If young pitchers master the use of the fast ball, curve, and change of pace, they may want to add other types of pitches to their repertoire. The slider is frequently used with good results by professional pitchers and can be taught to pitchers who have big enough hands to put strong pressure on the ball with their second or third finger, depending on how they want to spin the ball. However, a boy should not try to throw a slider without having an experienced pitcher or coach show him how to do it. The same thing is true of the knuckle ball—which is much more difficult to control—the fork ball, and other pitches.

HOLDING RUNNERS ON BASE. In pitching above the Little League level, pitchers must be taught to hold runners on base. If a runner steals a base, it is often the pitcher's fault for allowing the runner to get too big a lead. First he must become familiar with every facet of the balk rule, which every pitcher should memorize.

Proper control of the head can be very helpful to the pitcher. Peripheral vision will show him the distance the runner is from the base without a complete turn of the head. If the lead is too large, the pitcher should throw to the base. Veteran coaches claim that two successive throws to a base will tire out the runner who slides back to avoid a tag. Generally this will keep the runner from stealing on the next pitch.

Of equal importance with holding the runner close to his base is being able to maintain control and normal "stuff" in pitching to the batter from the "set position." The pitcher must be sure to fix his eyes on his target at home plate before he begins his pitching motion and to keep them there till the ball reaches its destination. The pitcher must keep in mind that he should begin his delivery only when he is relaxed and ready to pitch.

With men on base, it is advisable for the pitcher to change the timing between pitches in order to keep the base-runners from anticipating his moves. A clever pitcher like Preacher Roe or Lew Burdette will count to five before pitching one time, will count to 12 before pitching the next time, will count to three before pitching the next time, etc.

In pitching from the set position, a right-handed pitcher puts his right foot against the front of the pitcher's rubber and his left foot a comfortable distance in front of the rubber and slightly toward first when holding a runner on first base. When his objective is to hold a runner on second base, the left foot is more directly in line with home plate.

The left-handed pitcher places the left foot against the rubber, with the right foot a comfortable distance forward. The right foot is at an angle of almost 45 degrees toward first when he is holding a runner on first base and more directly in line with home plate when he wants to hold a runner at second base.

HIDE THE BALL. As the pitcher stretches, he may find that he can get better results by keeping more weight on the back foot although some pitchers prefer to keep the weight equally distributed on both feet. After raising the arms, with the glove hiding the ball from the batter, the pitcher must bring his hands to a position of rest in front of the body. The best rest position is slightly above the belt, with arms relaxed and glove still covering the ball. The ball must remain in the rest position for at least one second to avoid a balk, and the pitcher may throw to a base from the set position at any time. In throwing to first or third base he should be sure to have his eyes on the target before he throws.

In pitching from the set position, the pitcher shifts his weight to the back foot and pushes against the front of the rubber as he steps toward home plate with the front foot. Body action should be held to a minimum without taking away from the pitcher's normal "stuff." An exaggerated motion gives the runner more time to steal. He should keep his knee kick low and striding foot close to the ground. The arm and shoulder swing should be from second base to home plate with the same follow-through as used in the windup pitch, the pitcher hopping into a fielding position at the finish.

FIELDING THE POSITION. Being able to field his position is of great importance to a pitcher and his team. Pitchers must get into the habit of breaking for first base on any ground ball hit past them to the second-base side of the infield. If the first baseman attempts to field the ball, or does field it, and can't get back to the base in time to retire the batter, the pitcher should take the throw at first base. When the first baseman can get back to take a throw at first after fielding and throwing the ball to second base, the pitcher should continue on past the base to protect against an overthrow.

The pitcher should be on the alert and in position to cover any base left vacant in order to trap a runner between bases. On all throws from the outfield to home plate he should back up the catcher, and on throws to third base should back up the third baseman—being sure to back up deep enough to pick up the flight of the ball if it gets past its destination. When in doubt, he should run halfway between third and home and then break to back up the base to which the ball is thrown.

If the pitcher fields a ball, he should make his throw to the proper base as quickly and accurately as possible. Pitchers often delay too long in making the throw. Then if the baseman fumbles the throw, he doesn't have time to recover the ball before the runner reaches base.

The pitcher who traps a runner between bases should run at him with the ball to force the runner to break toward a base, keeping in mind whether there are other base-runners. If there is a runner closer to home plate, the pitcher must check to be sure that that runner doesn't advance a base before making a play on the trapped runner.

A pitcher must learn to keep out of the way of throws from the catcher to second base, as well as of throws between first and third base. Alert pitchers will drop to the ground when in the "line of fire" to give the thrower a clear view of his target.

PRACTICE DRILLS

There are many practice drills which can be helpful to a pitcher. Outlining the strike zone with cord and throwing a certain number of pitches at it from the regulation pitching distance every day can be very helpful. By keeping a record of the number of strikes and balls thrown from day to day, one can check on improvement in control. (See Figure 50.)

To make the drill more realistic, a teammate can be asked to stand behind the strike zone in his normal position in the batter's box. This will help him to improve his judgment of pitches and to become more familiar with the strike zone—at the same time giving the pitcher a more normal target.

When the pitcher's control improves so that he can throw the ball where he wants it to go two-thirds of the time, he can limit the target area by putting another string across it halfway between the top and bottom. Then he can concentrate on throwing all of his pitches into the lower half of the strike zone. When he gets so that he can do this with a high degree of consistency, he can practice throwing at the corners of the strike zone.

Professional pitchers frequently aim their warm-up pitches at the shoulders and knees of their catchers between innings of games. It is very important for the pitcher to aim at a definite target every time he throws a ball. A key factor in control is keeping the eyes on the target from the moment the windup begins until the ball reaches its destination.

The best way to teach a pitcher to field his position is to have him participate in regular fielding drills along with the other players. However, there are other methods, too. During batting practice, the catcher can be instructed to set up a play situation on every pitch not hit by the batter.

In the first situation, the manager or coach tells the catcher to roll, the ball down the first-base line the moment he catches it. The pitcher fields the ball and throws to first base. On the next pitch that isn't hit the catcher should roll the ball about halfway between first and second, slowly enough for the pitcher to be able to field it, and the pitcher throws to the shortstop covering second base. Then the catcher rolls the ball down the third-base line, the pitcher fielding it and throwing to third base. In tossing the ball down the base lines, the ball should roll about one-third to one-half of the distance to the bases since balls bunted that far should be fielded by the pitcher.

Other situations to set up occasionally include having the catcher toss the ball behind himself into foul territory. When this is done, the catcher retrieves the ball while the pitcher rushes in to cover home plate, takes the throw, and simulates the tagging of a runner coming in from third. Another play is that of tossing the ball in front of the plate for the pitcher to field and toss underhanded to the catcher as might happen in a squeeze-play attempt. The catcher also can toss the ball directly back to the pitcher to simulate the batted or bunted ball which is hit in that direction. Be sure that the catcher doesn't throw the ball too hard in this situation, particularly when working with young players.

In using this kind of drill during batting practice, limit the fielding drills to about one or two plays per batter. Otherwise the drill will drag on so long that it won't be beneficial to the batters. This type of drill works best when there is time for a lengthy practice session.

When pitchers are warming up, it is desirable to have a manager or coach present. The pitcher should warm up about 10 minutes. Then the coach should check to learn whether he is ready to throw hard.

He should begin with easy tosses and gradually increase his speed. After about five minutes, he can begin to spin the ball, if he includes breaking pitches in his normal pitching routine. It helps to throw three or four fast balls in a row, then three or four curves, a few change-ups or slow balls, etc. To avoid possible injury, the catcher should be advised before the pitcher throws him a different kind of pitch.

When the pitcher is warmed up and bears down, the coach should check to see that he grips and throws each pitch the same way, that he hides the ball, and that his motion doesn't tip off the type of pitch he is throwing. The pitcher should throw in the same direction during batting practice that he will throw during the game so that the wind resistance will be the same.

If a pitcher doesn't follow through properly, a helpful drill is to place a small stone or stick in front of the spot where he finishes his pitching motion. The pitcher should pick up the stone or stick as he finishes his follow-through. This can be repeated until the motion becomes part of his pitching pattern.

12

Fielding Drills

DUPLICATE GAME CONDITIONS. In conducting a fielding drill, the practice should come as close as possible to actual game conditions. A pitcher, for instance, cannot learn to participate in defensive maneuvers which involve him with other members of his team unless he practices with them in executing these plays. The reason a pitcher neglects to back up third base on a throw from the outfield, or fails to cover first base when the first baseman fields a ground ball to his right, or fails to field a bunt and throw accurately to second base in a force play or double-play situation is that the pitcher has no opportunity to practice these plays with most teams.

When managers and coaches of Little League teams in a dozen communities were asked to include their pitchers in every fielding drill, pre-game and otherwise, they reported the rapid improvement of their pitchers as fielders and the general improvement of defensive play by their teams. If a manager wants his pitcher for the game of the day to warm up in the bull pen during the fielding drill, he can place another pitcher on the mound for the drill. But be sure to provide fielding practice for every pitcher on the staff at regular intervals.

In the fielding drill the catcher should wear his mask, chest protector, and leg guards since he must field and throw while wearing them during games. (After several months of practice the catcher may not need to continue to wear all of his equipment, particularly on very hot days when the workout precedes a game.)

Keep in mind that you are trying to build confidence in your players. Try to hit balls they can handle easily.

WARM-UP A MUST. Be sure to keep in mind that your players should warm up their arms properly by throwing the ball at a short distance for at least five minutes before starting the infield drill. Youngsters want to start

Fielding Drills

throwing the ball hard and for a long distance the moment they get their hands on it. They can injure their arms if they are not required to warm up properly. In the outfield's fielding and throwing drills, managers should have their outfielders make practice throws to second base, to third base, and to home plate as warm-ups.

OUTFIELD DRILL

To begin the practice, have each outfielder field a fly ball and a ground ball and throw twice to second, third, and home bases. The throws to second base should be in the air and the throws from left field to third base should be on the fly. However, throws from right and center field to third base and throws from the outfield to home plate should be aimed at the cut-off man's head.

When the throws are from right and center field to third base, the shortstop should place himself about halfway between second and third and in line with the fielder and third baseman for each throw. Depending on his judgment of whether the throw could retire a runner attempting to reach third base, the third baseman will tell the shortstop to "Cut it off! Cut it off!"—shouting twice to be sure he is heard—or to "Let it go! Let it go!"

When told to "Let it go!" the cut-off man ducks or dodges the ball, which should be thrown so it will reach him on the fly and take one bounce to get to third base when he lets it go by. When told to "Cut it off!" the shortstop should catch the ball and make a practice throw to second base.

On throws to home plate from left field, the third baseman should line up between the fielder and home plate about one stride on the home-plate side of the pitcher's mound, with the second baseman covering second and the shortstop covering third.

On throws from center or right field, the first baseman is the cut-off man and should line up about one stride on the home-plate side of the pitcher's mound between the fielder and home plate. One throw from each fielder should be aimed at the cut-off man's head and the catcher will tell him whether to cut it off or to let it go. Like the shortstop on throws to third, he will dodge the ball when told to let it go, and will catch it and throw to second base when told to cut it off. The other throw from the outfielders to home plate should be on the fly if the fielders have strong arms to throw that distance. Otherwise they will be aimed at the cut-off man, too. A pitcher on the mound should back up third base and home plate on throws from the outfielders.

KEEP OUTFIELDERS BUSY. While the infield drill is taking place, a coach should be hitting fly and ground balls from the foul territory behind third base to the outfielders. He should alternate hitting the ball to their left, to their right, in front of, and behind them. He can have an extra pitcher or catcher catch the balls thrown in by the fielders.

INFIELD DRILL

PLAY FOR ONE OUT. 1. In the first round of infield drill, the play should be made to first base. The ball should be hit to the third baseman. The third baseman throws to the first baseman. The first baseman throws to the catcher, the catcher to the third baseman, and the third baseman back to the catcher.

In each case, the player who catches the ball should put the ball on the bag to simulate tagging out a runner who would be sliding to the base, before throwing the ball—unless the situation indicates a force play. In the case of a force play, the player who catches the ball should be sure to step on the base to complete the force before throwing the ball.

2. Continuing the first round, the ball is hit to the shortstop, who is playing at normal depth, and the shortstop throws to the first baseman who contacts the base while in possession of the ball and then throws to the catcher who throws to the shortstop who is covering second base where he tags the bag and throws back to the catcher who makes the tag again at home plate. The second baseman backs up the shortstop on all throws from the catcher when the shortstop normally would make the play at second base. The player who is backing up the base should be sure to be deep enough, at least 20 feet back of the base. In practice, have the player who fields the ground ball take the throw from the catcher.

3. The ball is hit to the second baseman who throws to first base, the first baseman to the catcher, the catcher to the second baseman at second base, and the second baseman to the catcher. On all throws to the bases the catcher should throw from in back of home plate because he will be required to do so in games.

4. The ball is hit to the first baseman who throws to the shortstop covering second base, and the shortstop throws back to the first baseman who touches the bag with a foot and then throws to the catcher.

The pitcher should break toward first base on every ball hit past him to the second-base side of the infield during the drill. On this play he should cover first base and take the return throw from the shortstop in case the first baseman can't get back in time. If the first baseman can get back to take the return throw the pitcher should run on into foul territory behind first base to protect against a possible wild throw or catching error.

PLAYERS KEEP INFIELD IN SIGHT. If the first baseman throws right-handed, he turns in toward the infield and pivots on the ball of his right foot, stepping with his left foot directly toward second base as he throws to second.

Fielding Drills

He should not pivot in such a way as to turn his back on the infield because in so doing he would take his eyes off his target and also lose sight of any baserunners who might be running on the base paths. With rare exceptions, he should turn so that the infield is in front of him at all times. If the first baseman throws left-handed, he does not have the problem of getting into position to throw to the other bases, but he too should always keep in mind that he should not turn his back on the infield. The only exception to this rule comes when an infielder goes into the outfield to catch a fly ball over his shoulder on the run. When possible, even on short flies to the outfield, the fielders should get under the ball and turn to make the catch with the infield in front of them.

5. Continuing the infield drill, the ball is tapped in front of the plate toward third base, where the catcher fields it with both hands and throws to first base. This throw should be made to the second-base side of first base with the first baseman stretching into fair territory to make the catch—avoiding any possibility of the ball hitting the runner who has bunted the ball and is running to first base. The first baseman then throws to shortstop covering second base, shortstop to third base, and third baseman to the catcher at home plate. Again, on these throws the player who catches the ball goes through the motions of the tag before throwing the ball—except at first base where "footing" the bag completes a force play. (There is very little chance for a first baseman to make a tag in Little League ball since the base-runner doesn't take a lead off the bag.)

6. The ball is bunted to the left of the mound so that the pitcher can handle it and throw to the first baseman who stretches for the putout at first and throws to the third baseman who simulates the tag and then throws to the catcher who makes the tag at home plate.

The second round of infield practice is a repetition of the first round except for the fact that the infielders should play deeper (at the edge of the outfield grass) and the ball should be hit harder to them for the long throw. The ball for the catcher to field should be bunted toward the first baseman who throws to third base, third baseman throws to second base, second baseman to first, and first baseman back to the catcher. The ball for the pitcher to field should be bunted to the right of the mound and the pitcher should throw to third base, third to second, second to first to home. On all long throws, the players should throw the ball overhand, with a backward rotation of the ball, because this throw will make the ball carry farther and make it easier to handle.

DOUBLE-PLAY ROUND. The third round should be a double-play round with the infield at normal double-play depth. Whenever the double-play situation is presented, the second baseman and shortstop must play closer to second base. In their regular defensive positions, they won't be able to make the play. Experimentation will determine how far they can play from the base and still make the pivot and throw. Most second basemen and shortstops find that taking a long step in toward home plate and one step toward second base brings them into the desired position. This is known as shading the bag.

1. The ball should be hit to the third baseman who throws to second base, the second baseman pivots on the bag and throws to first base, the first baseman to the catcher, catcher to third base to second base to first base to home. All throws to the pivot man on the double play should be aimed at his right shoulder. If he catches the ball "shoulder-high," it is much easier for him to complete the pivot and make the throw in one motion, and it increases the speed of the play—a very important factor in attempting the double play.

2. The ball is hit to the shortstop who throws to the second baseman who pivots at second base and throws to first base, to home, to the shortstop covering second, to third base, and back to home.

3. The ball is hit to the second baseman who throws the ball shoulder-high to the shortstop who touches second base and throws to first base, to home, to the second baseman covering second, to third base to home.

4. The ball is hit to the first baseman who throws to the shortstop at second base, shortstop throws back to the first baseman who "foots" first base and throws home; the catcher throws back to first base, and back to home.

5. The ball is tapped in front of home plate, the catcher fields the ball with both hands and throws it shoulder-high to the shortstop at second, shortstop throws to first, to home, to third, to shortstop at second, to first to home.

6. The ball is bunted toward the mound for the pitcher to field and throw to the second baseman who pivots at second base and throws to first base. The first baseman throws to the catcher, the catcher to the third baseman, and the third baseman back to the catcher.

DOUBLE PLAY THE HARD WAY. The fourth round is another double-play round, but more difficult play situations should be set up. Instead of the ball being hit directly at the fielders or to the side which will make the play easy, it should be hit to their far sides. In the case of the third baseman the ball should be hit to his right. He should then touch third base and throw to first base for the double play since with runners on first and second bases both outs would be force outs. In the case of the shortstop, the ball should be hit to his right, and in the case of the second baseman the ball should be hit to his left. In each instance the fielder should turn so that he has the infield in his line of vision at all times and make the throw to second base to start the double play.

The one other change involves the pitcher. The ball should be tapped to

Fielding Drills

his right so that he can field it and throw to third base for a force play, the third baseman stretching for the throw and then throwing to first base in an effort to complete a double play. The first baseman throws to the catcher, the catcher to the second baseman back to the catcher.

OPTIONAL ROUND. The fifth round is optional, depending upon the time allotted for infield practice. Managers may want to use it in Little League only when no game is scheduled for the day. However, all of the infielders should play deep. The batter should hit slow rollers so that the fielders will be forced to charge the ball and throw on the run. There are two other changes in this pattern. When the ball is hit to the first baseman, he should throw to the third baseman who touches third base and throws back to the first baseman at first base. The first baseman then throws to the catcher and the catcher back to the first baseman who goes through the motion of tagging a runner who has been caught off base and is sliding back. This tag should be made by placing the ball on the second-base side of the bag and letting the runner tag himself out as he slides back into the base. Then the first baseman throws back to the catcher to complete the round.

When the ball is tapped in front of home plate for the catcher to make the play, he throws to third base; the third baseman touches the bag and throws to first base, first base to home, home to third, to second, to first, to home. The ball is bunted to the pitcher's right, where he fields it and throws to first base, the first baseman to the catcher, the catcher to the third baseman, and the third baseman back to the catcher. If the fifth round is not used, the first baseman should throw to third base after fielding the ball on the second round of one.

BRINGING THEM IN. The last infield round is made with the infield drawn in for the force play at home plate. The ball is tapped to each fielder so that the fielder must charge the ball and throw the ball "knee high" to the third-base side of the catcher so that he will be in a position to tag the runner sliding into the plate. The routine is the usual one with the ball being hit to the third baseman who throws the ball to home plate, then to the shortstop who throws to the plate, then to the second baseman who throws to the plate, to the first baseman who throws to the plate, and finally bunted to the pitcher who throws to home plate.

This series of drills should cover a large majority of the plays an infielder is called on to make except for bunt situations.

If the team manager has plenty of time, he can include a round of infield practice which has the infield pulled in and the batter bunting the ball toward each infielder in turn and the fielder making the throw to first base. When the first baseman fields the ball in this situation, the second baseman generally covers first base and the shortstop covers second. Of course, there are bunt situations in which the pitcher covers first base, and some in which the first baseman makes the play at first unassisted. The drill to defend against the bunt should be conducted at a regular practice session along with other infield plays such as drills on pop flies and cut-off plays and relays from the outfield.

A final word of advice: encourage the infield to "talk it up" during the practice. Ample use of "chin music," the "old hubba hubba," or in plainer language "words of encouragement shouted at your teammates" during the workout will let your opponent know that you have a lively, determined, confident team. Talking it up has a tendency to relax your own boys when they might otherwise tighten up under the pressure of an important game.

SPECIAL SESSIONS. Special sessions can be scheduled involving the pitcher and catcher, with the pitcher making wild pitches, the catcher rushing back to the backstop to retrieve them, the pitcher running in to take the throw and make the tag at home plate.

13

Coaching and Signals

It is important to direct traffic on a baseball diamond, just as it is to do so on a city street if you want to get the proper results. The first- and third-base coaches are the "traffic cops" in a baseball game, and both the players and the coaches must know the signals if the traffic is to be handled properly.

BATTER WATCHES COACH. The moment a batter hits a ball, he should look toward the first-base coach as he starts to run. If the coach points toward second base, the runner knows that he should try for extra bases and govern his running accordingly. But if the coach waves him straight down the base line, he should not take a turn at first base, but should run as fast as he can down the line, because the play will be close at first base.

Going into second base, the base runner gets no help and is on his own. He must make up his mind from observation whether to slide, go into the base standing up, or try for an extra base.

SIGNALS AT THIRD. At third base, he will get plenty of help from the third-base coach. If he is to stop at third, the coach will have his hands in front of his chest with palms facing the runner. Once he has flashed this signal and the runner has seen it, the coach will bend over and push his hands toward the ground and to the right or left to indicate which way the runner should slide to avoid the tag. Or he will raise his hands over his head if the runner is to stand up.

If the runner has a good chance to score, the third-base coach will point toward home plate. Many coaches also use a whirling motion with the left arm in the direction of home plate to indicate that the runner should keep going.

ON-DECK BATTER COACHES. As the runner approaches home plate, he should depend on the next batter, who should be in the "on deck" circle, to tell him whether to slide or stand up. The batter will use the same motions as the third-base coach in telling the runner what to do.

FIG. 44. Ray Welsh, skillful coach of running, points his left arm toward second base as a signal for Bill Virdon of the Pittsburgh Pirates to continue to second base after reaching first safely on a base hit.

FIG. 45. By swinging his arm down the line and kicking his left foot in that direction, too, the first-base coach demonstrates that he wants the runner to continue straight down the line as he attempts to beat out an infield tap. Better running form would help the runner.

Coaching and Signals 117

FIG. 46. This is an excellent example of third-base coaching in the Little League World Series. The coach shows by his hands and arms that the baserunner is to slide to the outfield side of the base. Note the good slide by the runner and the good stretch by the third baseman for a low throw. The coach should swing his arms to the left with palms of hands down if he wants the runner to slide to the left.

FIG. 47. In this Little League Series game, the coach indicates that the runner is to continue to home plate by swinging his left arm in a circular motion toward home plate.

COACHING PRACTICE. During practice sessions early in the season, the manager can stand in the coaching box with his player-coaches and work with them on their assignments. Player-coaches can get as much benefit from a practice game as batters, fielders, pitchers, and catchers. The coaching box is an excellent place for them to learn the game, and alert and intelligent coaches can contribute much to their teams.

FIG. 48. This "on deck" batter-coach points to home plate to remind a home-run hitter to be sure to touch home plate as he completes his circuit of the bases.

OTHER SIGNALS. As players advance in baseball and the game becomes more complex, the signals too become more complicated. To hide them from the opposition, a catcher may use the customary finger signals, but doubling up the fist before or after the finger waving may mean that he will throw to a base or has called for a pitch-out. Some movement of his mitt, head, mask, or feet may mean that he has changed the signal for the kind of pitch he wants. Whenever there is any suspicion that the opponents may be picking up the signs, the catcher should change his signs without indicating to the opponents that he has done so.

It is helpful to the outfielders to know what kind of pitch will be thrown. Generally the shortstop flashes the sign behind his back and the second-baseman also can relay the sign since both are able to see the catcher's signs. Be careful that the opponents don't see them, too, or that some shift by an infielder or outfielder before the pitcher releases the ball tips off the opposition on what to expect.

The manager or coach may signal to his fielders whether to play deep or shallow, to the right or left, or to set up a special shift. However, there is no need to hide these signs, and he can do his signaling verbally if this seems

Coaching and Signals

desirable. The same is true when a manager wants his pitcher to give an intentional base on balls to the batter. He may want signs to tell the catcher what to throw to certain batters in crucial situations.

MANAGER RELAYS SIGNALS. With his team at bat, the manager usually relays the signs to the third-base or first-base coach, but he may have someone else on the bench do the actual signaling to cross up the opposition. Here are some signs John McGraw would relay to his New York Giants:

Team hit-and-run, with runner breaking on pitch: Player who gives sign holds bat between his knees.
Individual hit-and-run (use your own judgment on whether to try it): Arms folded.
Bunt for sacrifice: Scratches head.
Bunt for suicide squeeze: Rubs chin.
Bunt for safety squeeze: Pulls ear.
Steal: Bat on lap.
Take sign: Hand on knee.
Hit sign: Closed fist on knee.

As a rookie Frank Frisch taped a list of the signs in his cap and glanced at it whenever he had any doubt about what the sign meant.

The signs should be simple enough to be detected and remembered by your players, but complicated enough to avoid the peril of interception by the other team.

The most common signs used by coaches on the base lines for batters and runners are *flash signs*. These are flashed quickly by the coach and often

FIG. 49. The third-base coach has clenched his fists as a signal for the batter to bunt the next pitch as he shouts encouragement to him. Coaches should attempt to "pep up" their teammates.

are a combination such as one or two tugs at cap or hitch of belt; running hands across letters or brushing sleeve; and skin-to-skin such as rubbing hand on hand, arm, and neck. *Holding signs* are held longer for observation. Repeated clapping of hands, pointing toe toward batter, looking at first base, clenching fists, and a combination of both are typical examples.

In the matter of signals and signs, it is essential that everyone on the team understand the signs and that they have been received by the player to whom they have been relayed. Many teams have answering signs to indicate that they have been received and understood. When in doubt, call for time and carry the instructions in person to the player.

Some players tip off the signs by looking away the moment they read the signal. The player should keep his eyes on the coach for several moments after the sign has been flashed and the coach should continue to give dummy signals to avoid detection.

Signals and signs should be held to a minimum with young players. Don't confuse or overburden them with wigwagging that would startle the Signal Corps. A boy may have enough trouble in keeping his mind on the game situation without having to worry about a long series of signals. As Yogi Berra has said: "How can you hit and think at the same time?" Of course, this is an exaggeration, but don't keep a player from concentrating on the task at hand.

14

Training Aids

SLIDING AREA. The time to teach sliding is when a boy begins to play baseball. He is closer to the ground and eager to learn. Let the grass grow 6 or 8 inches high in foul territory at the end of a bullpen or outside the outfield fence. This is all the cushion the player needs.

If you can't grow grass in the area, spade up a pit 6 feet wide by 12 feet long and fill it with sand. This doesn't provide the same realism in movement as the grass, but will serve the purpose.

Place a loose (detached) base in the center of the sliding area. Every boy who is physically fit should practice sliding every time he goes to the field, sliding three or four times to the right and three or four times to the left so that he forms the correct habit pattern and has no fear of sliding. He should wear sliding pads, basketball trunks, or heavy swimming shorts to avoid skin burns.

Concentrate on teaching players to slide so that they land on the buttocks, where the body provides the most natural padding. It should be obvious that getting the arms and legs into the air will prevent possible breaks, sprains and chipped bones. Players should stay low when going into the slide and should keep in mind that it isn't a jump, but a slide. Once a boy learns this basic position, he can work on refinements such as the stand-up slide. Give a boy the chance to learn to slide and you may be amazed at the speed with which he masters the art.

PITCHING TARGET. The pitching strings, introduced to professional baseball by Branch Rickey, provide a target for a pitcher. Two strike zones are recommended. They are erected over home plates in the bullpen. (The bullpens, incidentally, should face in the same direction as the pitcher's mound and home plate.) They can be built of scrap lumber, painted white, and anchored to the ground with wooden pegs for this purpose. Poles 2 by 4 inches can be stuck into the ground approximately 10 feet apart with the

4-inch sides parallel to the pitcher's mounds. The poles should be lined up so that cords strung between them will be directly above the front of each home plate. One string should be at the average knee-high height of Little League batters and the other string at the average armpit height of a majority of batters in each league.

FIG. 50.   Pitching targets.

The strings, which can be obtained in hardware stores, should be of strong white cord similar to a carpenter's marking line. Once the cross-strings have been stretched, vertical strings at the width of each home plate should be strung between the cross-strings directly above the sides of a home plate to complete the strike zone.

Practice pitching mounds should be erected the proper pitching distance from the strike zones, and again practice pitching slabs can be built from scrap lumber, painted white, and anchored to the ground with wooden pegs.

When pitchers warm up, using the strike zone for a target, this practice can be made more realistic by having a batter stand in the batter's box. In this way the batter has a chance to judge strikes and balls and become familiar with the pitched ball, and the pitcher gets used to pitching to a batter.

After a few sessions, the batter can start his swing and then pull back to get the practice of checking his swing when the pitch is bad. This is a good drill for the batter, but he should never go through with the swing because it would break the strings and might injure someone working out elsewhere.

BATTING RANGE. If there is space near your playing field, develop a batting tee range. A net or canvas can be strung between poles or buildings. The size of the area is not too important, but an area from 8 to 10 feet high

Training Aids 123

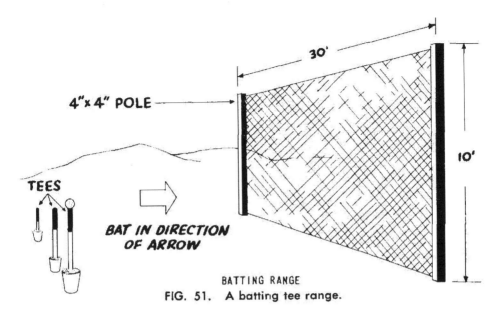

FIG. 51. A batting tee range.

and 30 feet wide is recommended. This would take care of three batting tees and batters at one time.

By using a woolen practice ball, the batting tee area could be set up beside a building or any other barrier which would eliminate the necessity of going a long distance to retrieve the batted ball. A woolen practice ball will carry far enough in flight to determine whether the batter is hitting line drives, grounders, or high flies, and will eliminate the breaking of windows and other hazards of that nature. Again if no area is available, tees can be set up behind the regular field backstop and balls can be hit against the backstop. Use a rubber-covered baseball, plastic ball, or tennis ball if woolen balls are not available.

The tees should be placed about 10 to 12 feet from the barrier so that the batter can determine by the flight of the ball whether he is hitting the ball on a line, which should be his aim, or hitting over or under it. A batter can also determine whether he is hitting to the opposite field, pulling the ball, or hitting straight away.

Batting tee "A" (see Fig. 52) can be built at very little cost by any parent for his son to use in the back yard, basement, or on the corner lot. It is constructed from a 5-gallon pail or can filled with sand which serves as the base, three varying lengths of broomstick, and a 6-inch length of radiator hose that serves as a seat for the ball. The three tees, or broomsticks, are cut to different lengths, as follows: (1) average knee height of the boy, (2) average waist height, and (3) average shoulder height.

Batting tee "B" (see Fig. 53) was designed by Arthur Dede for use at the

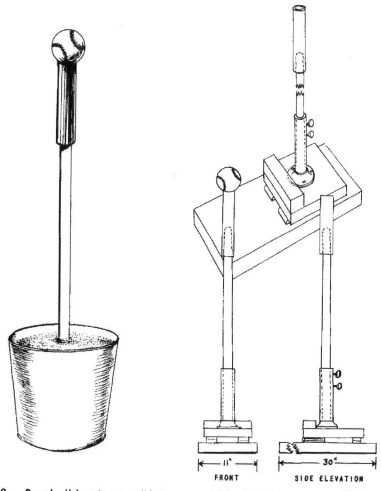

FIG. 52. Baseball batting tee "A."   FIG. 53. Batting tee "B."

Vero Beach spring training base by the Dodgers and their farm clubs. It can be built in any machine shop for approximately $15.

The baseboard should be rather rugged: say 30 inches long by 11 inches wide and 1 9/16 inches thick. The top board is about 9 inches wide, 12 inches long and 7/8 of an inch thick. An extra piece should be placed on the front end to serve as a bumper and also to reinforce the board. The two strap hinges can be 6 inches long and should be bolted on. The height of the top board, due to the hinges, should be the same both front and back. The distance in back can be made up with mending plates, which should be screwed on both top and bottom pieces. An extra piece of wood may have to be used as a spacer with the mending plates. These plates are also used as bumpers. The 1-inch pipe with the two thumb screws is 9 inches long and threaded on one end. The threaded end screws into a 1-inch flange, which is bolted through the top board, keeping the flange as far front as possible. The sticks in the pipe are broomstick handles (maple wood), and four sticks should complete a set: the lower one 12 inches long, the next one about 22, the third one about 34, and the long one about 44 inches. (Little Leaguers would not need the 44-inch tee, which is used only by adults to groove a swing for chest-high pitches.) As a rule the diameter of the sticks is about 7/8 of an inch so friction tape can be used to make up the difference and have a snug fit into a 1-inch piece of automobile radiator hose about 12 inches long. The piece of hose for the shortest stick is 9 inches long and fits on the broomstick handle about 3 inches. The three other pieces are 12 inches long and fit on the broomstick handles about 4 inches. The top of each piece of rubber hose should be chamfered with a razor blade to make a better seat for the baseball.

15

Fitness Isn't Seasonal

There is no substitute for daily exercise in building a strong, healthy body. Locomotive sports and activities such as walking, running, climbing, rowing, swimming, wrestling, and bicycling are valuable in keeping fit, and most experts agree that normal people should participate in this kind of exercise an hour each day.

Before beginning a physical fitness program, boys should be examined by their doctors. They should receive a medical check-up once a year and a dental check-up twice each year to detect defects or incipient diseases which may develop.

EXERCISES

There are many ways in which young athletes can keep physically fit the year round and thus improve their ability to play baseball and other athletic games. An excellent exercise is that of rope-jumping. Many athletic directors and basketball coaches use this exercise extensively for basketball players, and it is a favorite of professional and amateur boxers, wrestlers, and track athletes. Rope-jumping is highly recommended for developing agility, leg muscles, endurance, coordination, and rhythm, which are so important for baseball players.

Since research indicates that American boys are pathetically weak in the development of the upper shoulder girdle and since these muscles are so important in throwing and hitting, several exercises are recommended. One is rope-climbing, which helps to develop the upper shoulder as well as the biceps. To get the maximum benefit of this exercise, one should not slide down the rope, but lower himself hand-over-hand in the same manner as in climbing the rope.

Pull-ups also are very good for the development of the arms and shoulders. Young athletes should practice so that they can pull up their weight at least ten times.

Fitness Isn't Seasonal

FIG. 54. Rope climbing helps to develop the upper shoulder as well as the biceps. To get maximum benefit, lower yourself hand over hand in the manner in which you climb the rope.

FIG. 55. Pull-ups develop the arms and shoulders. Practice until you can pull up your weight at least ten times.

Strong wrists have great value to any athlete, and one way to develop wrist strength is to use bar bells or rods and to move them up and down with the wrists.

Finger strength can be developed by doing push-ups on the tips of the fingers, but this exercise should not be used before participating in a game or practice drill. It should be done at the conclusion of a workout or practice session. Another method of strengthening the hands is to carry a sponge rubber ball and to squeeze it frequently.

FIG. 56. Strong wrists are very valuable to an athlete. You can strengthen them by rolling bars up and down with the wrists as pictured here.

FIG. 57(a). You can make your own barbells by cementing broom handles into cans. Here cans are at the bottom of a wrist roll.

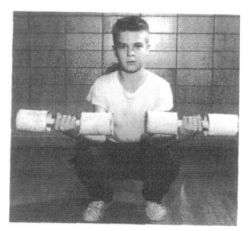

FIG. 57(b). Here he rolls up the homemade barbells.

Fitness Isn't Seasonal

Tumbling can be helpful in building coordination and balance. Individual gymnastic stunts such as forward and backward rolls, balancing on one leg and leaning as far forward as possible, doing a hand stand, and jumping in the air and spinning around to land facing in the opposite direction are helpful exercises.

FIG. 58. At the end of a practice session, you can develop finger strength by doing push-ups on the tips of the fingers.

Handball is an outstanding conditioner. Many of the arm movements are similar to throws in baseball, and both hands and arms are developed. You learn to stop and to go in a hurry, you make quick moves in all directions, gain strength and endurance, practice hand-eye coordination, learn to judge bounces off the wall as outfielders do and the hops of ground balls as infielders do.

Several college basketball coaches have discovered that the use of weights in an exercise can increase the leaping range of an athlete as much as three inches in a season. It doesn't take much imagination to see that increasing the jumping range of a player will permit him to spear more batted and thrown balls just as it will help him to shoot more baskets and block more shots in basketball.

The drill is simple—place a barbell, which is about one-third the weight of the athlete (if the player weighs 120 pounds, the barbell should weigh 40 pounds) on the shoulders of the player. Then have the player, in an upright position, raise up on the balls of his feet. Repeating this exercise daily and increasing the length of the exercise as strength is gained will give more bounce to the ounce. If barbells are unavailable, tie bags of rock or sand on the ends of a pole and they will serve the same purpose.

Another exercise which is of value in such sports as baseball, basketball,

FIG. 59(a). Again using regular barbells or homemade weights, try this exercise to increase spring in your legs. Start with weights on your shoulders which are one-third as heavy as you are (50 pounds if you weigh 150 pounds) and feet flat on the floor or ground.

FIG. 59(b). Then push up on the balls of your feet as high as possible and repeat this exercise several times each day, increasing the number of times as you gain strength.

tennis, and football is that of leaping to see how high one can touch on a wall. A boy will find that he can stretch higher by pulling one shoulder and arm down as the other goes up. The body is built that way. Again it will help him to leap higher and get more altitude with his glove to catch the ball. Barbells can also be helpful in this stretching exercise.

Learning to dribble a basketball, bouncing with one hand and then with the other, is good for hand-eye coordination, and shooting baskets develops agility, coordination, and balance.

Tossing a medicine ball will also build strength, but requires two participants.

There is no substitute for running and walking in conditioning a baseball player. Every boy should do as much of both as possible, and bicycle riding is a valuable exercise, too. Major league players—especially pitchers—have learned that strengthening their legs through running and walking is as important to their success as knowing how to pitch. That is why so many of them play golf, hike, walk, and trot throughout the year.

If the weather is so bad that he can'); get outside, a boy can find a place in a garage, barn, or basement where he can run "in place." In doing stationary running, he should be sure to lift his knees high, running from two to three minutes at a time. Ice skating and roller skating are valuable in strengthening legs, too.

Some people think that one can develop baseball skills only in the summer, but this isn't necessarily so. Coach Joe Bedenk of Pennsylvania State University has been one of the most successful coaches in college circles over a number of years despite the fact that the school is located in a cold weather belt and that his players do not have an indoor practice area.

The Penn State pitchers begin to throw outdoors in February, wearing high shoes and heavy "sweat suits." They walk in the snow to the practice bull pens under the partial shelter of one side of the football stadium. There they throw every day until the season opens, and one of the main reasons for the success of Bedenk's teams is the superiority of his pitching staffs. If a boy does throw in the winter months, he should not try to throw too hard and should wear warm clothes.

Of course the value of a batting tee is obvious in developing wrist action, in addition to improving batting form and performance. It can be used indoors or outdoors year round, hitting pressed wool, plastic, tennis, or rubber balls into nets, screens, or walls.

BUILD YOUR OWN. These drills and exercises can be done individually or in small groups. You can rig up a rope to climb by tying it to a tree branch, or the beam or rafter of a basement or garage. All you need for rope-jumping is a rope. For pull-ups, a tree branch, or two poles anchored in the ground with a rod stretched between them, or a broom handle tied at the ends with rope strung over a rafter will serve the purpose. An old mattress can be used for tumbling drills.

You can make your own bar bells by sawing off a broom handle to a length of about three feet, tacking nails into the ends of the handle and then cementing fruit juice cans onto the end of the handle. Patching cement works very well, and you can use larger cans to increase the weight as your wrists gain strength.

ADOPT HEALTH STANDARDS

Boys of Little League age, with a newly sprouting interest in physical prowess, will adopt health standards and habits that otherwise could not be imposed on them so thoroughly. This pattern can become a basis for life-long wholesome living.

Food is the source of energy. Unless a boy is abnormally underweight or run down, he doesn't need special dosages of vitamins. No matter how strenuously a youngster plays baseball, he'll derive enough energy from the well-balanced diet of the average American family.

Adequacy of diet is only part of the supervision Little Leaguers need from managers and parents. The habit of eating foods that are not good energy makers, though pleasant-tasting, must be corrected.

Dr. Erie V. Painter, official trainer of the New York Yankees for a dozen seasons, warns that since the Little Leaguer seems constantly hungry, between-meal snacks seem inevitable. But sweets, candies, cakes, super-duper whipped cream concoctions, and soda pop are not the best answer to this legitimate hunger. Taken in large amounts, sweets sate the appetite for other foods. Between-meal snacks should be energy-making and appetite-refreshing. Sandwiches with meat, cheese, or honey; milk (thought of as a food rather than as a drink); and fruits and fruit juices are preferable.

Food digestion is slowed during heavy physical activity, and players should not drink copiously of water—especially ice water. Do not chill the stomach with icy drinks immediately after eating because it slows down digestion. Drink water only in very small amounts while exercising. It is preferable to rinse your mouth when it is dry and then to spit out the water. Train yourself not to drink until after you have cooled off, and then to drink slowly. It's a good rule not to eat immediately before or after exercising.

All fine athletes know how to relax, even during a game. To relax doesn't mean being without tension. Instead, it is the elimination of unnecessary tension. The basic technique of effective physical performance is: "Start from rest; tense only when necessary; return to rest." Relaxation can be developed in everyday functions like eating, breathing, playing, and going to sleep.

Fitness Isn't Seasonal

Here's what Dr. Henry Donn says about sleep, in his health column of the *Scholastic Coach* magazine:

> Judging by the amount of sleep they get, some youngsters think that it's a waste of time. Sleep is vital to good health. It builds, creates new spirits, readies you for the next day's tasks. Loss of sleep has a bad effect upon the nervous system as well as on the general appearance. Though your muscles can rest and renew their strength while you are awake, your nervous system cannot. During every waking hour there's an expenditure of nervous energy. So make sure to get at least nine hours of restful sleep per night.

Dr. Ray Duncan recommends as much as 10 hours of sleep a night for boys of Little League age. The amount of sleep needed varies with the individual, but most athletes sleep longer than nonathletes since they need to store up energy.

In the general realm of health habits, athletes should include the following: if you can't brush your teeth after every meal, at least rinse out your mouth with water. Wash hands and face before eating and before going to bed. Shampoo your hair at least once a week. Keep fingernails clean. Guard against infection by promptly washing with soap and water any break in the skin and then cover with a clean bandage. Remember that tobacco and alcohol cannot help an athlete to become physically fit.

And a final tip from Dr. Painter:

> Leg and arm strains are the most common injuries in baseball. Proper conditioning and proper warm up will help you to avoid these injuries. If pitchers are physically fit and warmed up properly before bearing down, and if they throw naturally, they won't get a sore arm by throwing hard. Keep the arm warm and relaxed between innings. Use liniments sparingly; once in condition you have practically no need for them. If you are bothered by a recurrent sore arm, ask your coach to watch you pitch to see if he can detect a hitch in your delivery.

16

An Education Helps

Some boys who give their school work the "once over lightly" treatment might change their attitudes if they realized that every school is a school for athletes. That there are many boys with athletic aptitudes who don't "bear down" in the schoolroom seems to indicate that additional or different motivation might be helpful in keeping these lads interested in the learning process.

The examples of a Branch Rickey or a George Sisler point up the importance of an education to the athlete. Mr. Rickey, responsible for more changes in baseball than anyone else, has an excellent educational background, including degrees from Ohio Wesleyan and the University of Michigan. He has used his education to excellent advantage in becoming the outstanding teacher of baseball; he has the scholar's approach to the sport. After nearly sixty years of experience he still searches eagerly for new methods of teaching the fundamentals, for new ideas about testing the abilities of players and improved techniques to develop their talents, and for better procedures in playing the game.

Mr. Rickey keeps an open mind and an open door for every man with an idea, but it is his educational background which enables him to separate the practical ideas from the crackpot schemes, and to explain to the "idea men" why their plans do or do not have merit.

George Sisler, perhaps Mr. Rickey's prize pupil and one of the great players of all time, is a graduate of the University of Michigan with a major in engineering who has applied his training in engineering with positive results to playing, coaching and scouting. Sisler is regarded as one of the finest coaches in the game because of his ability to analyze a situation and to describe methods of getting more mileage out of a player's skills.

Contrast these men with a major league pitcher blessed with a great physique but hampered by meager education. The president of the club

An Education Helps

told the player, "The difference between big money and peanuts in baseball is in taking care of yourself."

"I've been wrong," admitted the player. "I've made a lot of mistakes but I want to be a good pitcher."

The president smiled as he said, "I'm glad you used the past tense. I believe . . ." The pitcher interrupted, "Look, mister, I've been wild out there a lot of times, but I've never been tense."

Studying English helps a player to express himself properly and to understand what others are saying to him on and off the athletic field. The effective use of language is priceless when the choice of the right word or expression helps to keep a situation under control. In public speaking, English is invaluable to an athlete constantly in the public limelight. A command of English has been the difference between a player becoming a manager or being unemployed at the end of his playing days; it always is a determining factor in his long-range success.

Knowing foreign languages helps eliminate the language barrier, especially now that baseball and other sports attract men from various countries. With Luis Aparicio and Chico Carrasquel of Venezuela, Bobby Avila of Mexico, Orlando Cepeda, Bob Clemente and Ruben Gomez from Puerto Rico, and nearly a dozen Cuban natives starring in the major leagues today, the ability to speak Spanish is an asset to any player. Al Campanis, a graduate of New York University, is aided considerably as a baseball scout after hanging up his spikes and glove because of his ability to speak Spanish. He roves through Latin America recruiting promising prospects for professional baseball.

THE VALUES OF SCHOOLING. Anything that a boy learns in school helps him in one way or another to become a better athlete. Obviously physical education teaches him how to condition himself, to know which exercises develop certain skills and when and where to use them. It teaches him that exercises, beneficial in one sport, may not be desirable in another, and that under certain conditions mixing such sports as baseball and swimming does not achieve the best results. Physical education also covers the use and care of equipment, the treatment of injuries, and general first aid.

Health and hygiene classes deal with the amount of sleep required and when rest can be most advantageous, the kinds of food to eat, and when and how to eat them in order to gain strength and stamina. The saga of baseball is filled with stories of talented players who "ate themselves out of the league."

Perhaps less obvious is the value of physics and its applications to baseball. The boy who knows that a low center of gravity helps to maintain balance, and who learns how to control his center of gravity, has the advantage over one who doesn't know these things.   This is particularly true in fielding a ground ball, and in getting a quick start while running bases. Physics deals with pressures, rotations, and grips that give the ball its direction in flight, not to mention the fact that a ball released at eye level is easier to control. The angle of the bat and the batting stance also are explained by a knowledge of physics, and leverage and the law of action and reaction enter the picture, too.

Naturally mathematics comes into the picture, particularly with the player who wants to take advantage of percentage play. To the professional player, ability to handle money becomes doubly important; and the study of law surely can be helpful in negotiating contracts, interpreting the rules of the game, and transacting other business connected with a baseball career, whether it be as an amateur or professional.

Arts and crafts are of value because a player may want to mend or reshape, lace or replace, the lining in his glove or other equipment. Players have been known to reshape bats to their individual tastes on a lathe. These skills lay the foundation for pleasant and satisfying hobbies for the athlete during his leisure.

One cannot overestimate the value of psychology to a team or player. It teaches the athlete how to encourage his teammates, the attitudes that are desirable, and the ways to achieve cooperation and team play. In fact, the application of psychology to sports is almost unlimited.

There are epic examples of how psychology works to advantage or disadvantage of a team. Many baseball fans remember the case of Bill Terry who, when manager of the New York Giants, asked if the Brooklyn Dodgers were still in the league, and then saw the Dodgers spurred on to blast the Giants out of pennant contention.

Fresco Thompson, now a vice-president of the Los Angeles Dodgers, recalls his days as captain of the Philadelphia Phillies when they were perennial "cellar-dwellers." In the words of Fresco, "We were down so deep that only on a clear day could we see seventh place." Fresco remembers that opposing players, not wanting to shake the Phils out of their lethargy, were most solicitous and thoughtful about the health and welfare of the Philadelphia players. If a Phils batter hit the ball hard, opponents were sure to let him know that he looked good and that he certainly was having tough luck, thereby leaving the impression that if the Phils had to lose at least it wasn't so bad to lose to such kind, considerate fellows!

PSYCHOLOGICAL LESSON. Another illustration of a psychological lesson is provided by a minister, the Reverend Gordon Thompson:

> During my spring vacation I went to see some baseball games. One night, in a game between the New York Yankees and the Chicago White Sox, I saw the complete history of a small hate complex—its origin, its growth, and its results.

An Education Helps

The New York pitcher was fast, but like many fast-ball pitchers, he had trouble in controlling the ball. In the early innings he hit two of the Chicago batters and missed three or four others by inches—accidentally, I believe.

Apparently the man he found it hardest to pitch to was an infielder. The first time he came to bat, the pitcher hit him in the side. Two innings later, when the infielder came to bat again, he had to drop to the ground twice to avoid inside pitches.

Quite understandably, the batter was annoyed. He "got on" the pitcher. When he shouted uncomplimentary remarks, we could not distinguish the words in the stands but we could imagine their general meaning.

The second time the Yankee pitcher came to bat, the infielder decided to get even with him and to teach him a lesson. When the count was one ball and one strike, he called for time and came in from his position to talk to the Chicago pitcher. Some of us in the stands sensed that what he was saying to the pitcher was, "Dust this guy off, and do it good—for me!"

I am not sure, of course, that this is what the infielder said—but what happened next looked like the answer to such a request. The White Sox pitcher, whose control was good that evening, threw the next ball high and inside, and the Yankee pitcher fell away fast from a pitch that was going to miss his nose, if it did miss, by a fraction of an inch. Back at his defensive position, the infielder waved his gloved hand in the air in apparent satisfaction. The count was now two balls and one strike. The pitcher threw again. And again the pitch was high and inside—and this time the Yankee pitcher dropped to the ground to dodge the ball. Up went the infielder's arm again, and he shouted something like, "Pour it at him, boy!"

But the count now was three balls and one strike. On the next pitch, the pitcher missed the plate—accidentally. So the Yankee pitcher walked, and later in the inning scored a run.

Now here is the point of this baseball parable. The score of the game at the end of nine innings was 4-4. In the tenth inning New York scored another run and won. If the White Sox pitcher hadn't walked the Yankee pitcher, Chicago would have won the game in nine innings, 4-3. So the infielder got his revenge. With the help of his pitcher he paid back the Yankee pitcher —and thereby lost the ball game.

In more important areas of life than sports contests, and sometimes with more indirect but equally catastrophic results, our hatreds defeat us in the attainment of our essential purposes.

Of course, the study of citizenship can have a great influence for good in the field of sportsmanship and in setting a pattern of conduct for future athletes to follow. A book could be written about games lost by players whose unfair tactics aroused their opponents to fight back, or about prejudiced debates with umpires which did not change the umpire's decision but caused the removal of players, coaches, and managers from the contest. Battling the umpires is never a constructive pastime and, in its more extreme essence, constitutes rebellion against the laws that govern the game and thus against the game itself. Habitual umpire-baiting is a form of anarchy. When decisions of judgment are made, it is morally and ethically constructive to accept them.

Every school subject prepares for the next one from the first day of school until the student completes his formal education. And the whole learning process has a related value to baseball. From this standpoint, perhaps teacher preparation offers the greatest opportunity to the participant. In order to become a teacher, he must learn how to teach; and to become a coach, he must learn how to coach. The player who can analyze the fundamentals and tactics of the game and who teaches them to another improves his knowledge in the process and enhances his ability to play.

There are hundreds of ways in which these and other subjects apply in improving the skills and attitudes of the boy who wants to play baseball or participate in any team sport. It is safe to conclude that everything else being equal, *the educated athlete is the best athlete and the one who gets the most enjoyment from participation.*

17

Setting an Example

Hero worship seems to be inherent in the human race, and a particularly strong factor in determining the behavior of young people, who pattern their actions after those of their heroes. For this reason the physical prowess of Biblical heroes like King David and Peter, the big fisherman, has captured the imagination of people, as have ancient Greeks like Ulysses and Hercules, or Richard the Lionhearted of England who wielded a two-handed sword with one hand. Similarly the mental, moral, and physical strength of such American heroes as George Washington and Abraham Lincoln continues to set an example.

Hero worship is especially common at younger age levels, where beginners look up to the better players on the teams and try to emulate them. Thus responsibility must go with ability, and players must be taught the importance of setting a good example on and off the field. The attitudes and actions of managers, coaches, umpires, officers, parents, and other spectators create a climate of sportsmanship, citizenship, and constructive living and provide patterns which young players can be expected to follow.

CODE OF CONDUCT. With alert and sympathetic guidance, boys will develop healthy codes of conduct. Several years ago a team from Portland, Maine, was participating in the Little League World Series. One of the officials spoke to the boys about the importance of setting a good example and displaying responsibility. He pointed out that they should be enthusiastic in their play and have fun while playing, but that they must be on guard against saying or doing things which would set a bad example for young onlookers.

Later these boys were guests at a professional baseball game. They sat near one of the dugouts, where some of the language used by the players was far from saintly. After the game, several of the Portland Little Leaguers approached the official who had talked to them earlier about responsibility.

One of the boys spoke up: "Did you hear the swearing at the game tonight? It was awful. Those men weren't living up to their responsibilities."

The Portland boys had learned a lesson which should be learned by everyone in baseball. The game will grow and prosper only as long as it produces heroes like Christy Mathewson, Lou Gehrig, Pepper Martin, Walter Johnson, George Sisler, Honus Wagner, Peewee Reese, Alvin Dark, Phil Rizzuto, Bobby Brown, Al Rosen, George Kell, Gil Hodges, Carl Erskine, and Stan Musial—to name but a few—who did and do live up to their responsibilities.

As one example of their responsibility, a newspaperman once asked Honus Wagner to endorse a certain brand of tobacco, pointing out to Honus that the tobacco company would pay both of them for the endorsement. Wagner thought over the proposal and then wrote to the newspaperman. He stated that he didn't smoke and didn't think smoking was good for athletes, and for that reason he would not endorse tobacco. However, he added that he realized that the newspaperman had a large family and needed money, so he was enclosing a personal check payable to the newspaperman for the amount he would have received if Wagner had endorsed the tobacco.

The following check list may be a helpful reminder to all concerned.

RESPONSIBILITIES

MANAGER AND COACH:

To inspire in his boys a love for the game and the desire to win.

To teach them that it is better to lose fairly than to win unfairly and to stress the values derived from playing the game fairly.

To lead players and spectators to respect the integrity and judgment of officials by setting them a good example.

To be the type of man he wants his boys to be.

To eliminate all possibilities which tend to destroy the best values of the game.

To show cordial courtesy to opposing teams.

To achieve a thorough understanding and acceptance of the rules of the game and the standards of eligibility.

To encourage leadership, use of initiative, and good judgment by the players on the team.

To recognize the aim of the game to promote the physical, mental, moral, social, and emotional well-being of the individual players.

To remember that an athletic contest is only a game—not a matter of life or death for players, coach, official, fan, state, or nation.

Setting and Example

PLAYER:

To live clean, to play hard, and to play for the love of the game.

To win without boasting, lose without excuses, and to continue to strive despite defeat.

To respect officials and accept their decisions.

To always remember that he represents his family, team, league, community, and country.

THE UMPIRE:

To know the rules.

To be fair and firm in all decisions. To call them as he sees them.

To treat players and coaches courteously and demand the same treatment for himself.

To know the game is for the boys and to let them have the spotlight.

THE SPECTATOR:

Never to boo a player or official.

To appreciate a good play no matter who makes it.

To know that the team, league, and community get the blame or the praise for his conduct.

To recognize the need for more sportsmen, and to strive to set an example of fair play in every thought and action.

EVERYONE INVOLVED:

> To live the Little League pledge:
>
> I trust in God,
> I love my country and
>   will respect its laws,
> I will play fair and strive to win-
>   But win or lose,
> I will always do my best.

Index

Aaron, Hank, 44
Abranis, Cal, 69
Accident insurance, 13
Accident prevention, 10, 12-13
Aparicio, Luis, 19, 27, 48, 74, 135
Ashburn, Richie, 28, 69
Athletics, 19
Attitudes, of players, importance of, 5-6, 139-40
Avila, Bobby, 135

Balls
  curve, 101-102, 103
  fast, 94, 96, 100
  fly, catching, 70
  fork, 104
  ground
    infield play, 54-55
    outfield play, 71
  knuckle, 104
  screw, 101
  slow (change of pace), 100-101
Barbells, use of, 128, 130, 132
Barrow, Ed, 21
Baseman, *see* First baseman; Second baseman, Third baseman
Base-runners
  breaking from bases, 26, 28
  coaches aid to, 115-20
  rounding bases, 25-26
  rules for, 28-29
  and sliding, 29-33
  tagging, 57
Base-running drill, 29
Bases
  blocked, avoiding, 32
  breaking from, 26, 28
  leading off, 27
  rounding, technique for, 25-26
  stealing, 27, 28, 104
    stopping a double steal, 63, 87
  tagging up at, 27
Bats
  choking, 42
  taping handles of, 42
  weight of, 41-42
Batting, 34-47; *see also* Bunting, Hitting
  ability, testing, 17-18
  drills, 42-47
  follow through, 41
  fundamentals, 39-42
  in the box, 47
  order, 48-50
  practice, 38-39, 41, 42-47
  stance, 39-41
  stride, 41
  swing, 41
Batting tee, 44-46, 122-25
Bedenk, Joe, 131
Bender, Chief, 19
Bent-leg slide, 31, 32
Berra, Yogi, 21, 46, 76, 77, 120
Brown, Bobby, 140
Brown, Mordecai "Three-Finger," 90
Bunn, John, 10
Bunning, Jim, 89
Bunting, 34-39
  drills, 46
  for base hit, 37-38
  practice, 38, 39
Bunts
  catcher's play, 83
  defensive play, 57
  drag, 37, 38
  fake, 34-35
  push, 37, 38
  sacrifice, 35, 38
Burdette, Lew, 98, 104
Burk, Mack, 87

Capability, of players, adjusting to, 54
Campanella, Roy, 19, 21, 22, 45, 76, 87
Campanis, Al, 135
Cardinals, 20, 62, 63
Carey, Max, 28, 48
Carrasquel, Chico, 135
Catchers
  bunts, handling, 83
  fielding drills, 108
  low pitches, blocking, 83
  pitchers aided by, 86-87
  plays at home plate, 83-85
  position for catching, 79
  requirements, 20, 76
  selecting, 77-78
  shifting for pitches, 81-82
  signal squat, 78, 79
  signals, 78-79, 120
  stance, 79, 80, 81
  target for pitchers, 80-81
  throwing ability, testing, 16
  throwing hand, 81
  throwing to bases, 82-83
Catching, 76-88
  drills, 87-88
  fundamentals, 78-88
  habits, good, 76-77
  low pitches, 83
  pop flies, 83, 87
  position for, 79
  stance, 79, 80, 81
Center fielders, 71
  requirements, 20
Cepeda, Orlando, 135
Change of pace, 100-101
Clemente, Bob, 135
Coaches, 115-20
  first-base, 115
  on-deck batter, 115, 118
  responsibilities of, 140
  third-base, 115, 117, 119
Coaching, 115-20
  practice, 118
Cobb, Ty, 23, 42
Conduct, code of, 139-41
Colavito, Rocky, 20
Coombs, Jack, 19
Cooperation, importance of, 6, 51
Criticism, 8
Cross-over pivot, 58-59, 62-63
Cubs, 21
Curve ball, 101-102, 103
  overhand, 102
  sidearm, 102

Cut-off plays
  on throws to home plate, 64-65, 85
  on throws to third base, 65

Dark, Alvin, 35, 140
Dean brothers, 89
Dede, Arthur, 123
Deras, Art, 69
Dickey, Bill, 19, 77
DiMaggio, Joe, 19, 23, 25, 68
Disciplinary problems, dealing with, 9
Dodgers, 19, 21-22, 30, 43, 44, 45, 52, 69, 74, 76, 77, 101, 124, 136
Donn, Dr. Henry, 133
Donovan, Dick, 38
Double-play, 57-63
  cross-over pivot, 58-59, 62-63
  drag, 61
  drills, 111-13
  rocker pivot, 58-59
  shortstop inside base path, 60
  shortstop outside base path, 61-62
Double steal, stopping a, 63, 87
Drag bunt, 37, 38
Drag pivot, 61
Dressen, Charlie, 35
Drills
  batting, 42-47
  bunting, 46
  catching, 87-88
  fielding, 108-14
  infield, 110-14
  pitching, 106-107
  outfield, 75, 109-110
  running, 23
Drysdale, Don, 89
Duncan, Dr. Ray, 133
Dunne, Bert, 44
Durocher, Leo, 54

Earnshaw, George, 19
Education, importance of, 134-38
Eisenhower, Dwight D., quoted, 11
Erskine, Carl, 69, 92, 140
Esslinger, Arthur A., 10
Evaluation, of players, 18
Exercises, physical, 126-31

Fast ball, 94, 96, 100
Fielding, *see* Infield play; Outfield play
Fielding drills, 108-14
  infield, 110-14
  outfield, 109-10
Finger strength, developing, 127, 129
First-Aid kit, 13

Index

First base, playing, 65-67
First-base coach, signals used by, 115, 116
First baseman
  requirements, 20
  technique for, 65-67
Fitness, physical, program for, 126-33
Flash signs, 119-20
Fly balls, catching, 70
Follow through, batting, 41
Food, proper, 132
Force plays
  catcher and, 85
  infield positions and, 57
Fork ball, 104
Ford, Whitey, 89
Fox, Nellie, 19, 44, 49, 50
Frisch, Frank, 119
Furillo, Carl, 20
Fundamentals, importance of learning, 10-11

Gehrig, Lou, 140
Giants, 19, 47, 101, 119, 136
Gilliam, Jim, 38, 74
Glasses, use of, 16, 78
Gomez, Lefty, 68, 89
Gomez, Ruben, 135
Goodman, Billy, 38, 50
Gordon, Joe, 19
Gowdy, Hank, 83
Grip, pitcher's, 91-92, 93
Ground balls
  infield play, 54-55
  outfield play, 71
Grove, Bob, 19

Hale, Dr. Creighton, 97
Handball, as a conditioner, 129
Head-first slide, 32
Health
  habits, development of good, 9
  standards, 132-33
Heckling, 8
Herman, Billy, 58
Hero worship, 139
Hitters, testing, 17-18
Hitting; *see also* Batting, Bunting
  line drives, 46
Hodges, Gil, 20, 21, 43, 44, 45, 140
Holding signs, 120
Hole, throwing from the, 15-16
Home plate
  catcher's plays at, 83-85
  cut-off play on throws to, 64-65, 85

Hook slide, 30-32
Hoover, Herbert, 3
Hornsby, Rogers, 25, 47
Hubbell, Carl, 21, 101
Hustling, need for, 7-8

Infield drill, 110-114
Infield play, 51-67
  bunts, 57
  double-play, *see* Double-play
  double steal, stopping a, 63
  force plays, 57
  fundamentals, 54-57
  ground balls, 54-55
  moving sideways, 55
  preparation for, 51-54
  run-down plays, 63-64
  shifting with hitters, 55-57
  tagging runners, 57
  target for throws, 57, 63
  throwing, 15-16, 55, 61-63
Infielders
  fundamentals for, *see* Infield play
  requirements, 19-20
  technique for, *see* Infield play
  testing, 17
  throwing ability, testing, 15, 16
Insurance, accident, 13

Japan, attitude toward baseball in, 6, 69
Jay, Joey, 100
Jeffcoat, Hal, 21
Johnson, Walter, 21, 140
Judgment, importance of, in base-running, 27-28

Kaline, Al, 20, 44, 68
Kell, George, 140
Kluszewski, Ted, 42, 46, 49, 50
Knuckle ball, 104
Kuenn, Harvey, 44, 70

Landis, Jim, 49
Larker, Norman, 74
Leaders, importance of knowing players, 4-5
Leadership, 3-11
Left fielders, requirements, 20
Lemon, Bob, 21
Line drives, hitting, 46
Loes, Billy, 98
Lollar, Sherman, 19, 49, 50, 77
Lopat, Eddie, 21, 89
Lopez, Al.. 48, 50

Macias, Angel, 90
Mack, Connie, 19, 51
Maglie, Sal, 21
Mamaux, Al, 43
Managers
   responsibilities of, 140
   signals used by, 119
Mantle, Mickey, 23, 35, 42, 44
Marion, Marty, 61, 62
Martin, Pepper, 20, 140
Mathewson, Christy, 140
Mays, Willie, 23, 27, 28, 44, 68, 70
McAnany, Jim, 50
McCraw, Lynn, 6
McDougald, Gil, 97
McGraw, John, 19, 119
Medical examinations, 13
Miller, Eddie, 54
Mitchell, Clarence, 101
Moon, Wally, 38
Moser, Clarence G., 9
Musial, Stan, 23, 35, 42, 44, 46, 140

Neal, Charley, 17, 42, 74

On-deck batter coaches, 115
Ott, Mel, 20 Outfield drill,
109-10 Outfield play, 68-75
   adjusting to situation, 68-69
   backing up the infield, 74
   drills, 75
   flies, catching, 70
   fundamentals, 70-75
   ground balls, 71
   learning, 71-74
   position for, 71
   preparation for, 52
   throwing, 70-71, 74-75
   traffic control, 71
Outfielders; *see also* Center fielders; Left fielders; Right fielders
   requirements, 20
   technique for, *see* Outfield play
   testing, 17
   throwing ability of, testing, 15
Overhand curve ball, 102 Over striding, 24

Pafko, Andy, 22
Painter, Dr. Erie V., 132, 133
Phillies, 136
Phillips, Bubba, 50
Physical fitness program, 126-33
Piersall, Jim, 68

Pirates, 24, 25, 116
Pitchers
   aided by catchers, 86-87
   automatic, 46-47
   breaking pitches, 101
   choosing, 16-17
   control by, 89-91, 98-100, 106
   drills for, 106-107
   fielding position, 105, 106
   fielding practice, 108
   holding runners on base, 104
   requirements, 21, 89
   stance, 105
   taking signals, 96-97
Pitching, 89-107
   breaking pitches, 101
   control, 89-90, 98-100, 106
   curve ball, 101-102
   drills, 106-107
   fast ball, 94, 96, 100
   fundamentals, 91-106
   grip for, 91-92, 93
   motion, 97-98
   requirements, 21
   slow ball (change of pace), 100-101
   target, 121-22
Pitching machine, automatic, 46-47
Pitch-outs, 27, 28
Pitching strings, 121-22
Piurek, John, 42
Pivot, double play
   cross-over, 58-59, 62-63
   drag, 61
   rocker, 58-59
Plank, Eddie, 19
Players
   attitudes of, importance of, 5-6
   capabilities of, adjusting to, 54
   championship, 19
   development of, 9
   evaluation of, 18
   leader's knowledge of, importance of, 4-5
   medical examinations, 13
   responsibilities of, 141
   skills, use of, 38
Podres, Johnny, 98
Pop flies, catching, 83, 87
Pull-ups, 126, 127, 131
Push bunt, 37, 38
Push-ups, 127, 129

Razzing, 8
Reese, Peewee, 19, 21, 22, 28, 52, 54, 140
Reiser, Pete, 35
Relax, development of ability to, 132

Index

Reynolds, Allie, 89
Richards, Paul, 20
Rickey, Branch, iii, 3, 19, 21, 23, 43, 44, 77, 88, 89, 121, 134
Right fielders, requirements, 20
Rivera, Jim, 50
Rizzuto, Phil, 19, 23, 54, 140
Robinson, Aaron, 77
Robinson, Jackie, 19, 21, 22, 23, 24, 26, 28, 38, 39, 45, 58, 88
Rocker pivot, 58-59
Roe, Preacher, 89, 104
Rommel, Ed, 19
Rogovan, Sol, 21
Rope-climbing, 126, 127, 131
Rope-jumping, 126, 131
Roseboro, Johnny, 77
Rosen, Al, 42, 140
Run-down plays, 63-64
   practicing, 87
Running, 23-29
   ability, importance of, 15, 21-22, 23
   breaking from bases, 26, 28
   drills, 23, 29
   in foul territory, 25
   judgment in base-running, 27-28
   rounding bases, 25-26
   rules for base-runners, 28-29
   tips on, 23, 24
Ruth, Babe, 21

Safety, 12-13, 31
Score, Herb, 97-98
Screwball, 101
Second baseman, 56
   in double play, 58-59
   requirements, 20
Shantz, Bobby, 89, 98
Shaw, Bob, 77
Sheehan, Tom, 101
Sherry, Larry, 98
Shortstop
   choosing boy for, 15
   making double play, 60-63
   requirements, 19
Sidearm curve ball, 102
Signals
   catcher's, 78-79, 96-97, 118
   first-base coach, 115, 116
   manager's, 119
   on-deck batter coaches, 115, 118
   third-base coach, 115, 117, 119
Signs
   flash, 119-20
   holding, 120

Sims, Joey, 90
Sisler, Dick, 69
Sisler, George, 21, 23, 90, 134, 140
Skinner, Bob, 24
Slaughter, Enos, 69
Sleep, need for, 133
Slider, 104
Sliding, 29-33
   avoiding a block, 32
   bent-leg slide, 31, 32
   head-first slide, 32
   hook slide, 30-32
   practice, 121
   stand-up, 32
Slow ball, 100-101
Smith, Al, 49
Snider, Duke, 19, 22, 35, 45, 69
Spectators, responsibilities of, 141
Speed, of players, importance of, 21-22, 23
Spring tryouts, 14-18
Sprinting, 23, 24-25
Stance
   batting, 39-41
   catcher's, 79, 80, 81
   pitcher's, 105
Stand-up slide, 32
Stengel, Casey, 48
Stirnweiss, George, 91
Stolen bases, *see* Bases, stealing
Stride
   batting, 41
   lengthening, 23-24
Sun field, catching balls in, 75
Swing, batting, 41

Tagging runners, 57
Tagging up at a base, 27
Target
   for pitcher, 80-81, 121-22
   for throws, 57, 63
Team, building a, 19-22
Tee, batting, 44-46, 122-25
Terry, Bill, 136
Third base, cut-off play on throws to, 65
Third-base coach, signals used by, 115, 117
Third baseman, requirements, 20
Thompson, Fresco, 46, 136
Thompson, Reverend Gordon, 136
Throwing
   ability, testing, 15
   by infielders, 15-16, 55, 57, 61-63
   by outfielders, 70-71, 74-75
   from the hole, 15-16
   in the double play, 57-58
   target for, 57

Toporcer, George, 51-52
Training aids, 121-25
   batting range, 122-25
   pitching target, 121-22
   sliding area, 121
True blood, Elton, 3-4
Try out program, spring, 14-18
Tumbling, value of, 129
"Two-way" lead, 27, 28

Umpires, 91

  attitude toward, 5-6

  responsibilities of, 141

Versatility, of players, 21-22
Virdon, Bill, 25, 116

Wagner, Honus, 23, 54, 140
Warm-ups, importance of, 108-109, 133
Walters, Bucky, 21
Weights, use of, 129-130
Welsh, Ray, 24, 116
White Sox, 19, 38, 42, 48, 49, 50, 74. 77, 136-37
Wilhelm, Hoyt, 21
Williams, Ted, 25, 44
Wilson, Jimmy, 28
Wrists, strong, development of, 127, 128
Wynn, Early, 89

Yankees, 19, 132, 136-37

Also available from www.sunvillagepublications.com...

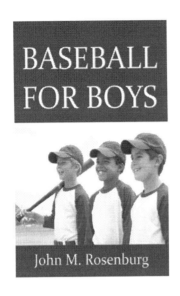

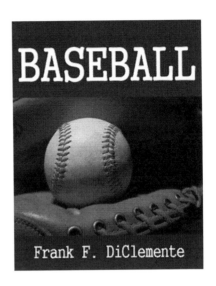

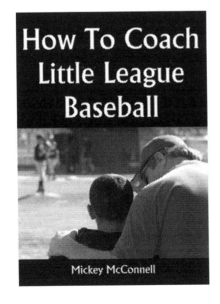

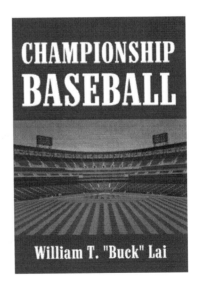